SUPER Simple Designs II

An Easy Coloring Book for Everyone

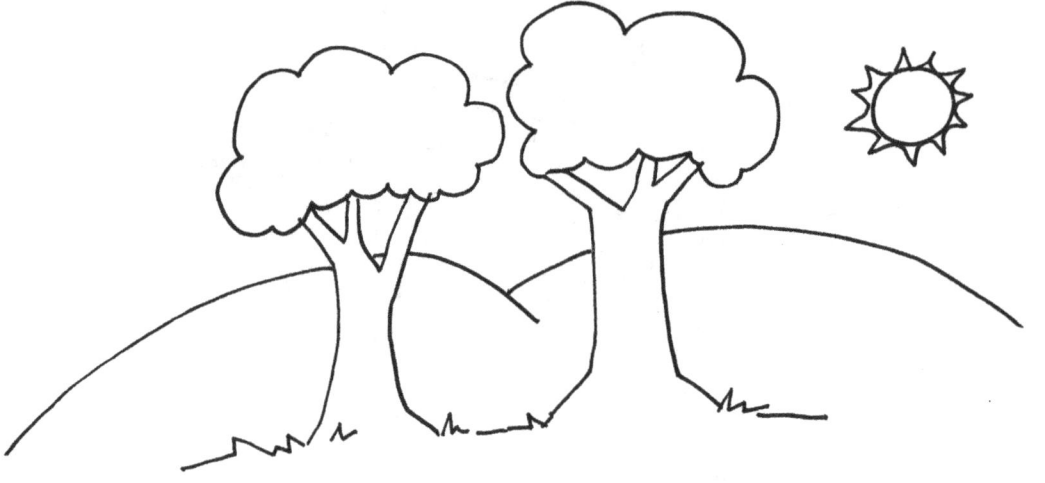

By Kimberly Garvey

Cover Drawing By Kimberly Garvey

Cover Drawing Colored By Donna Pecoraro

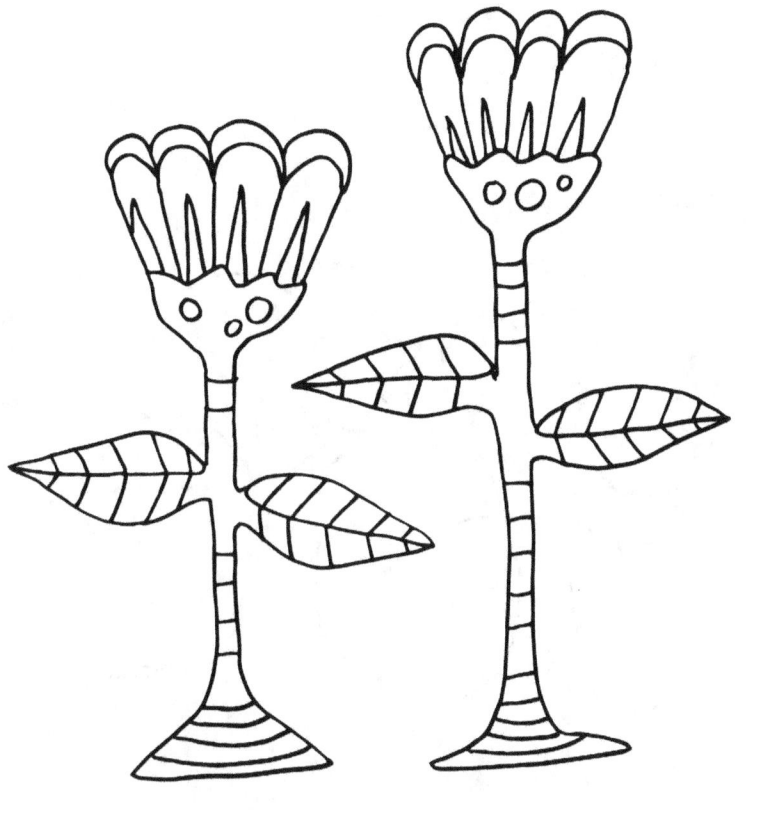

Smiling Bat Productions

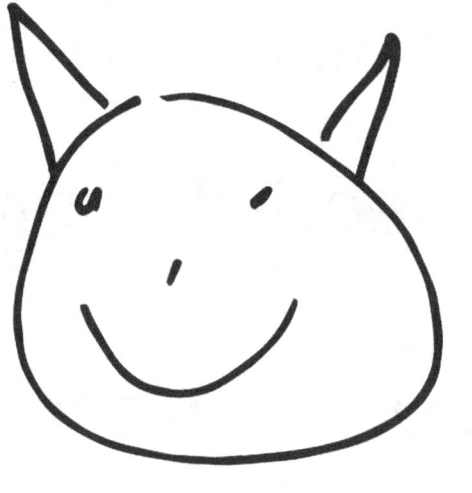

This book is dedicated to everyone I love.

WARNING!!!!

Please put a protection sheet of paper between the pages when using markers to prevent bleed-through.

A protection sheet is included at the back of

this

book.

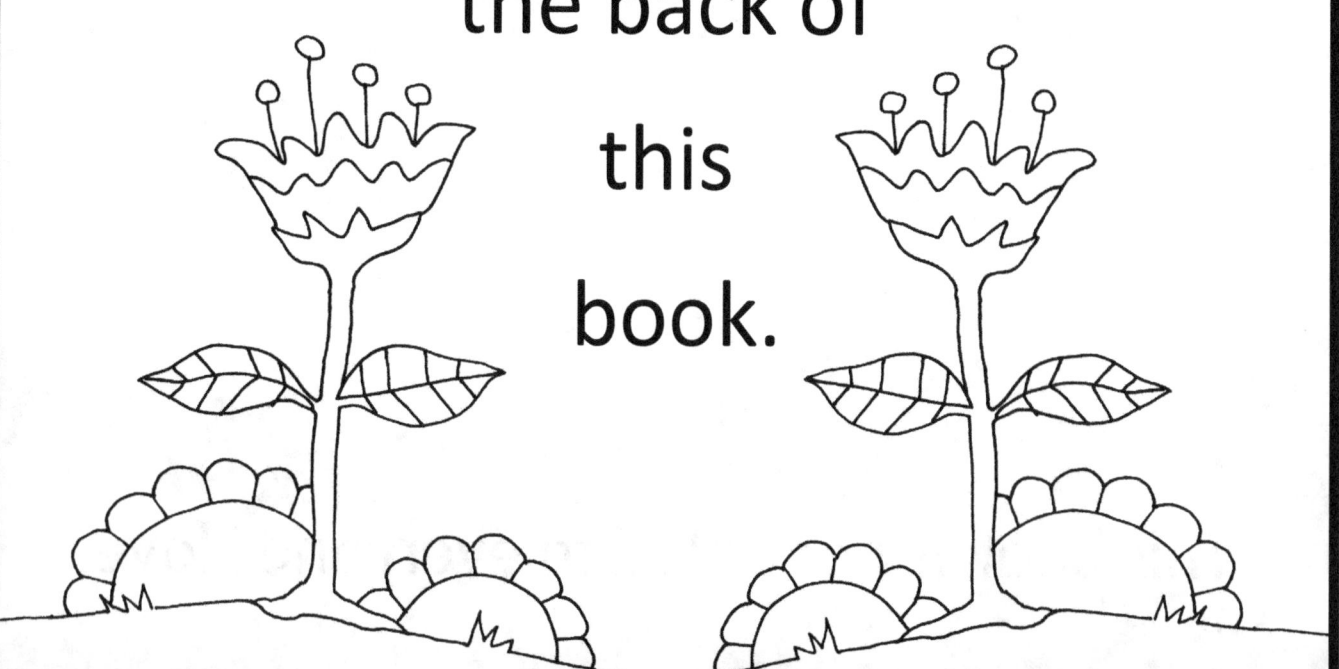

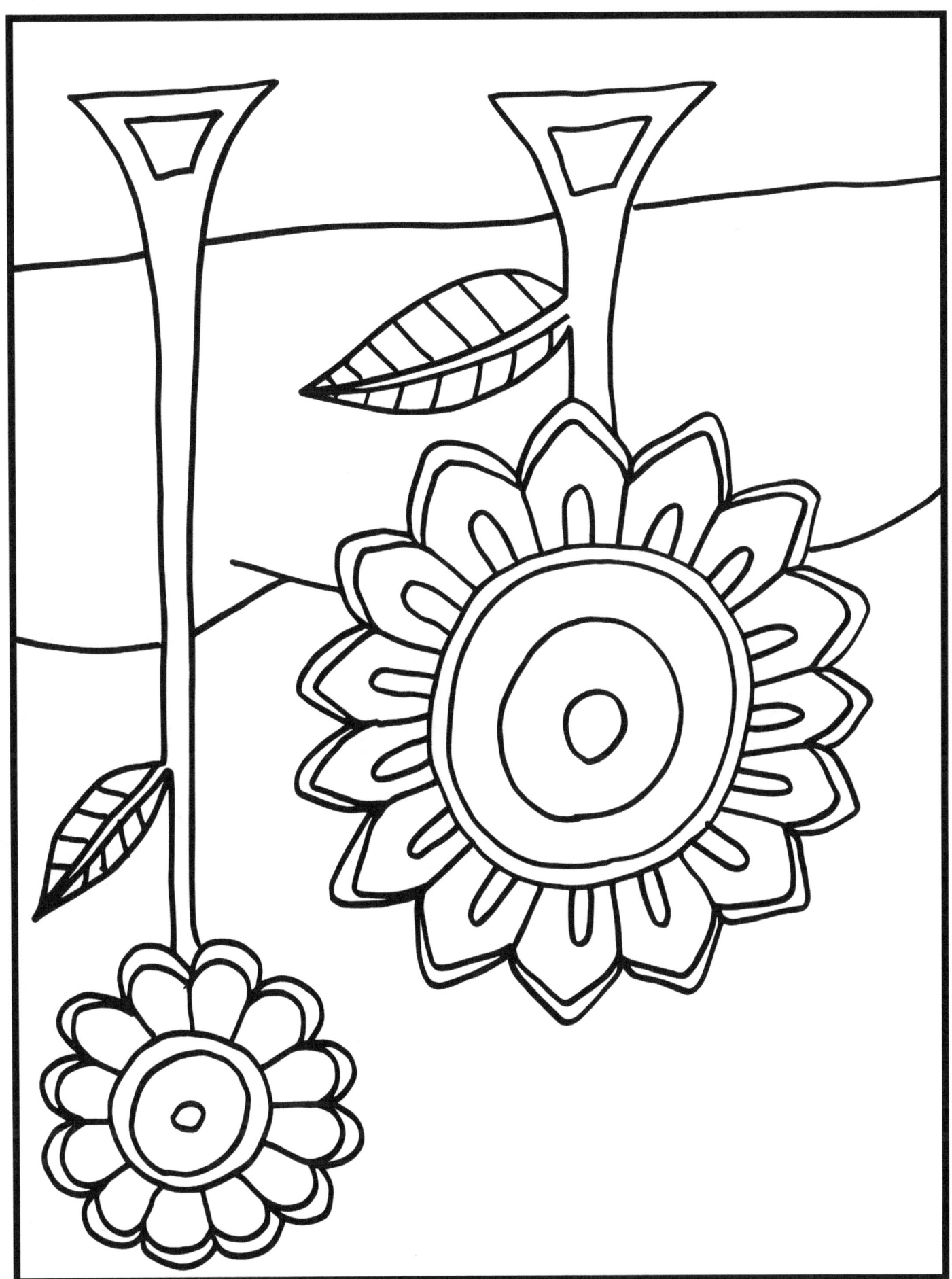

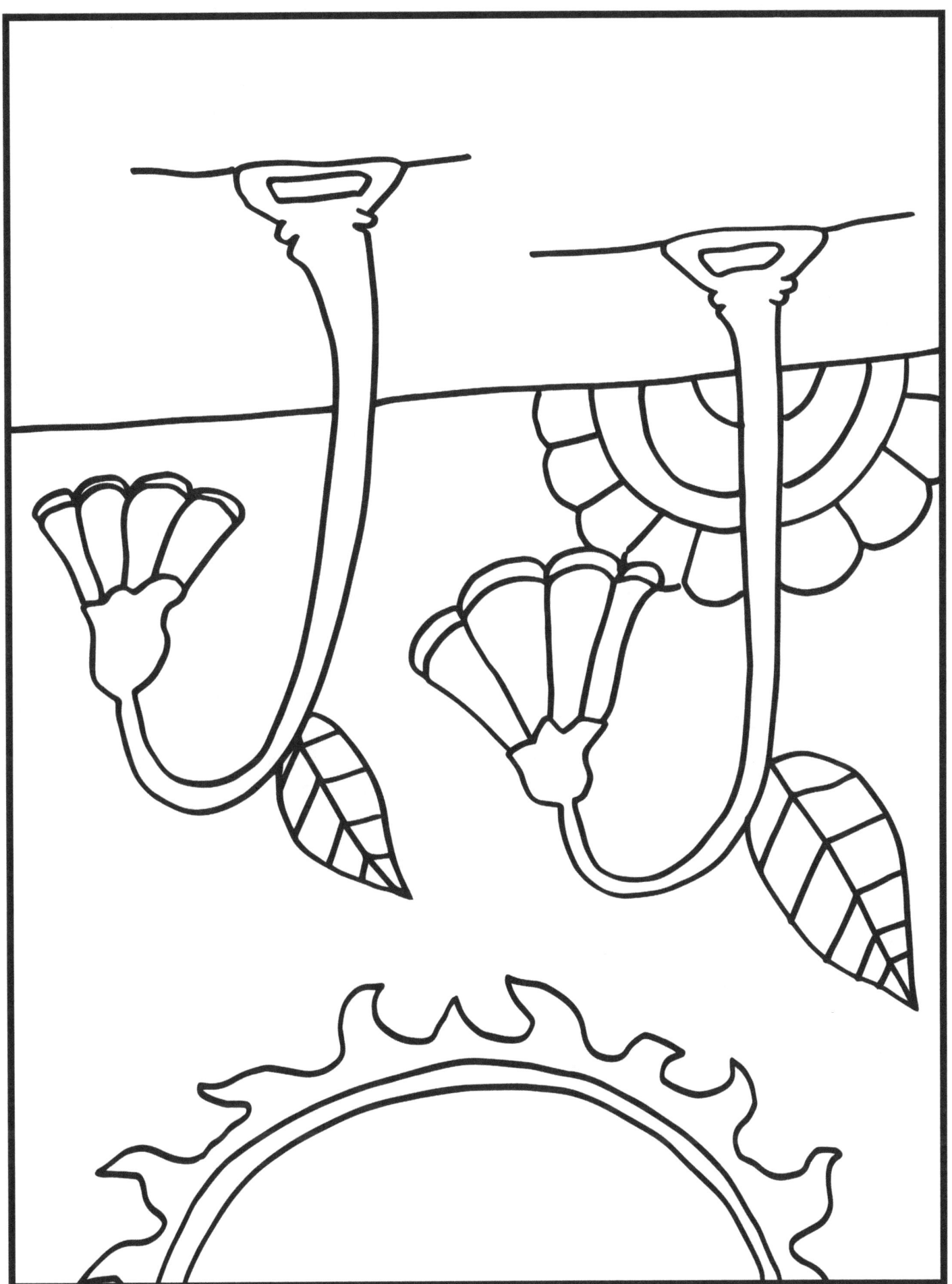

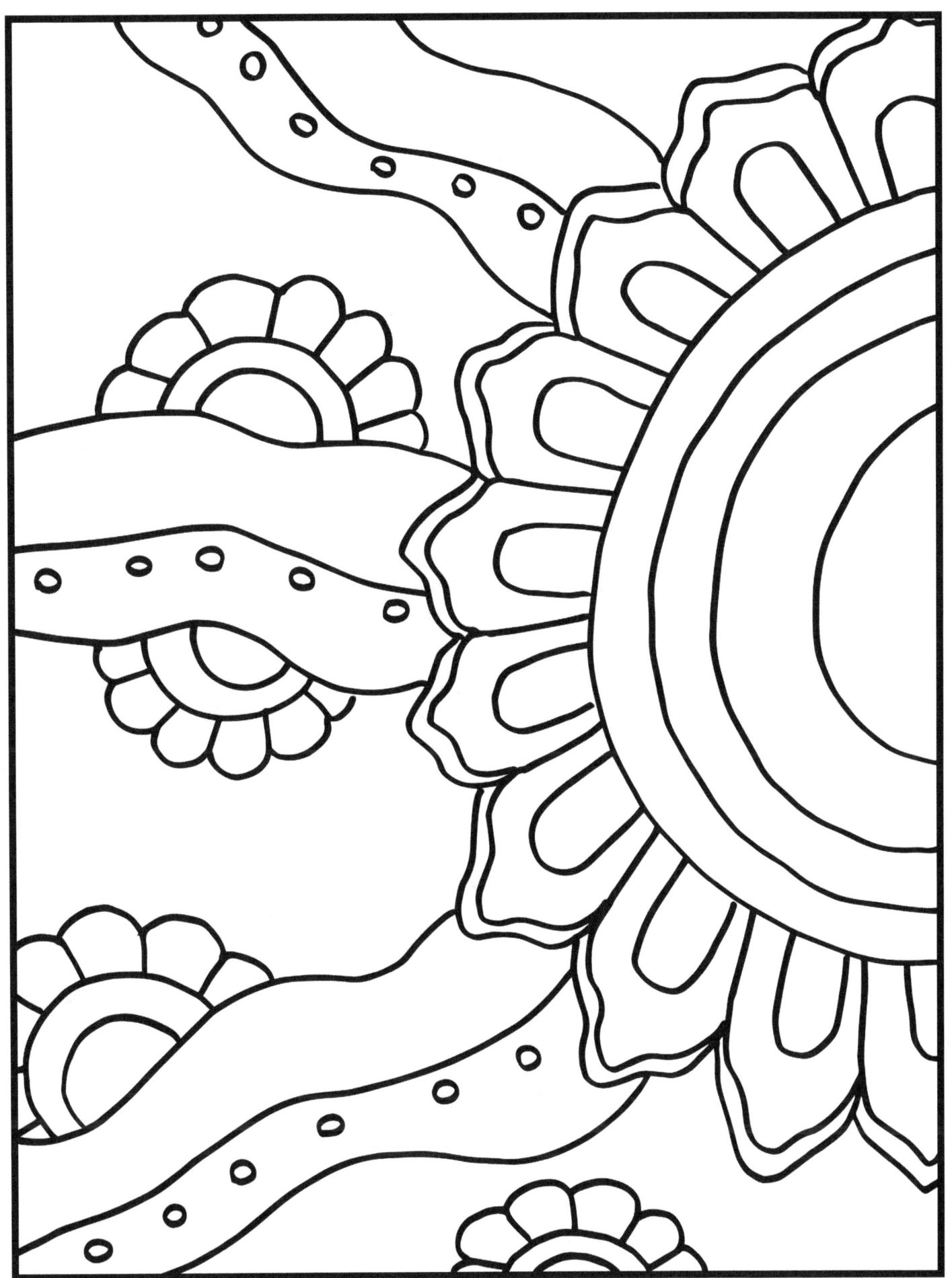

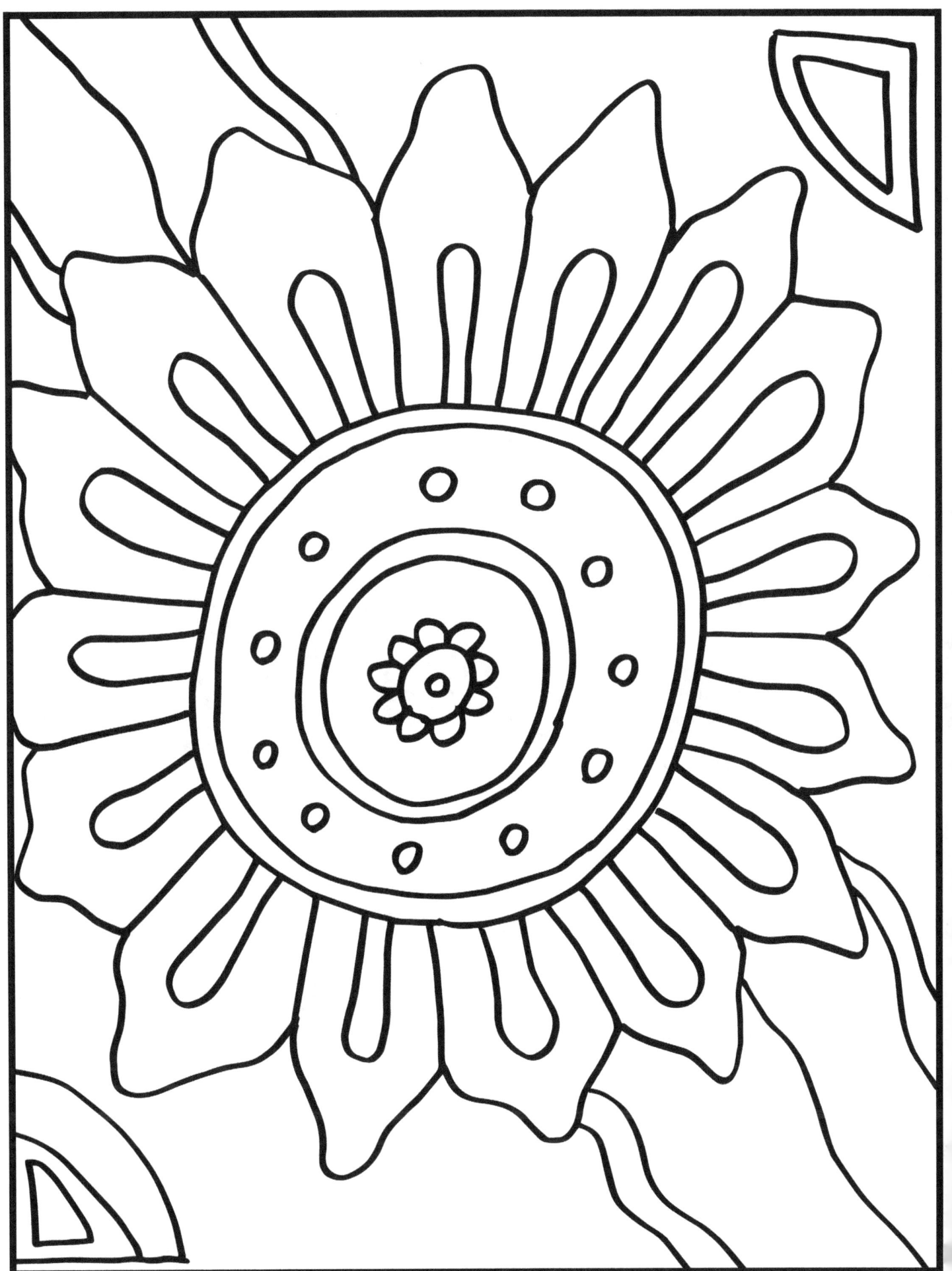

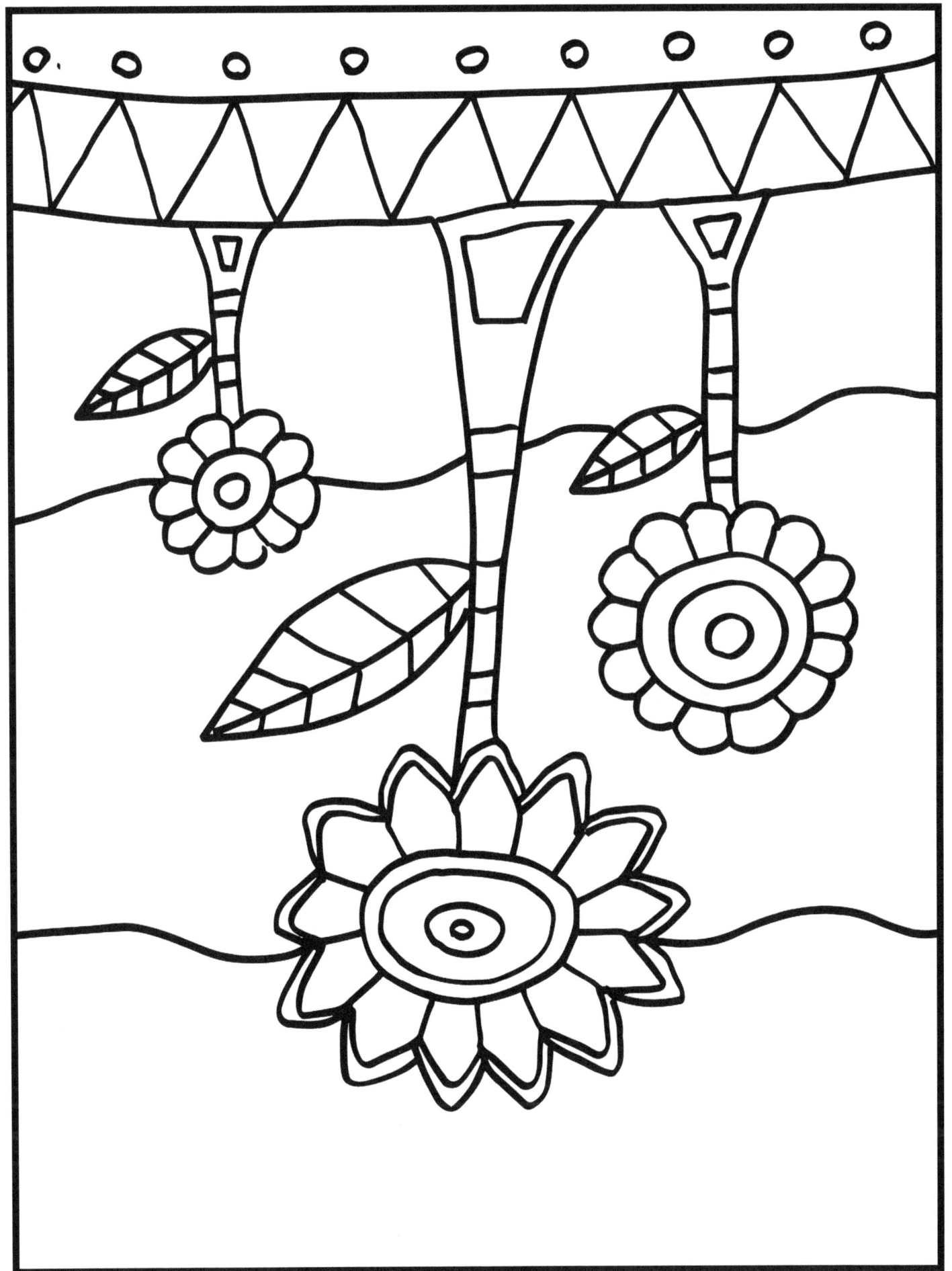

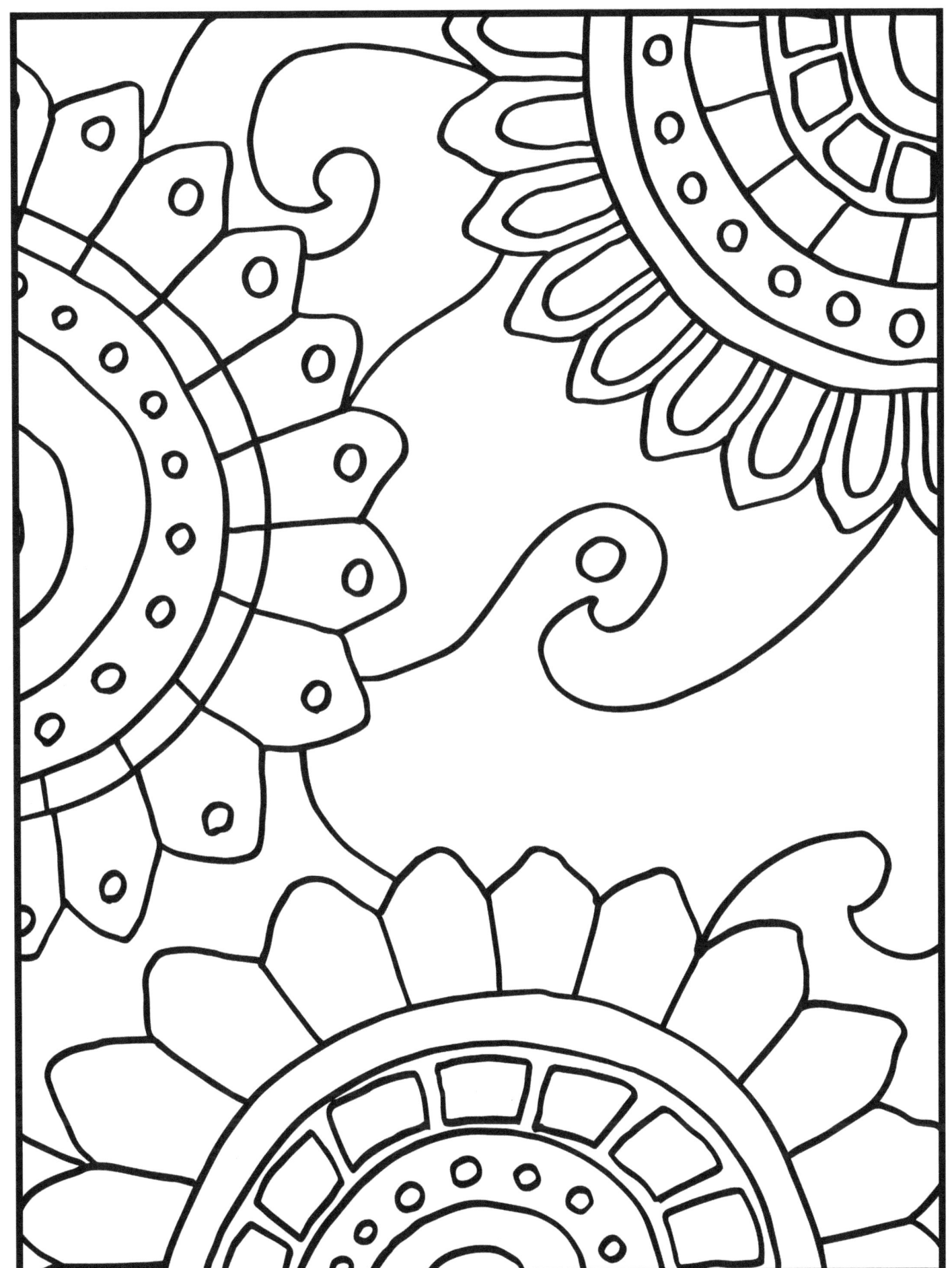

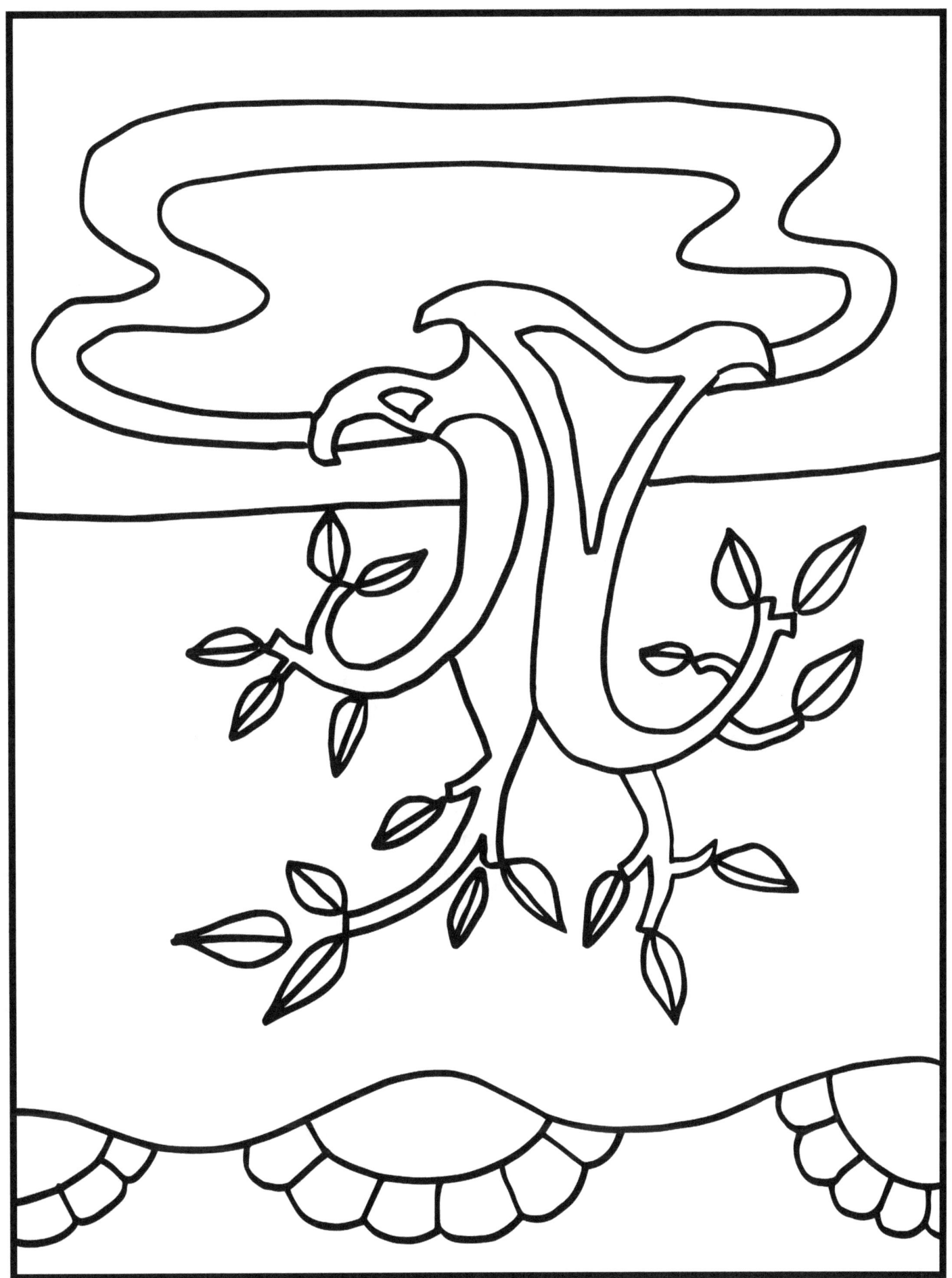

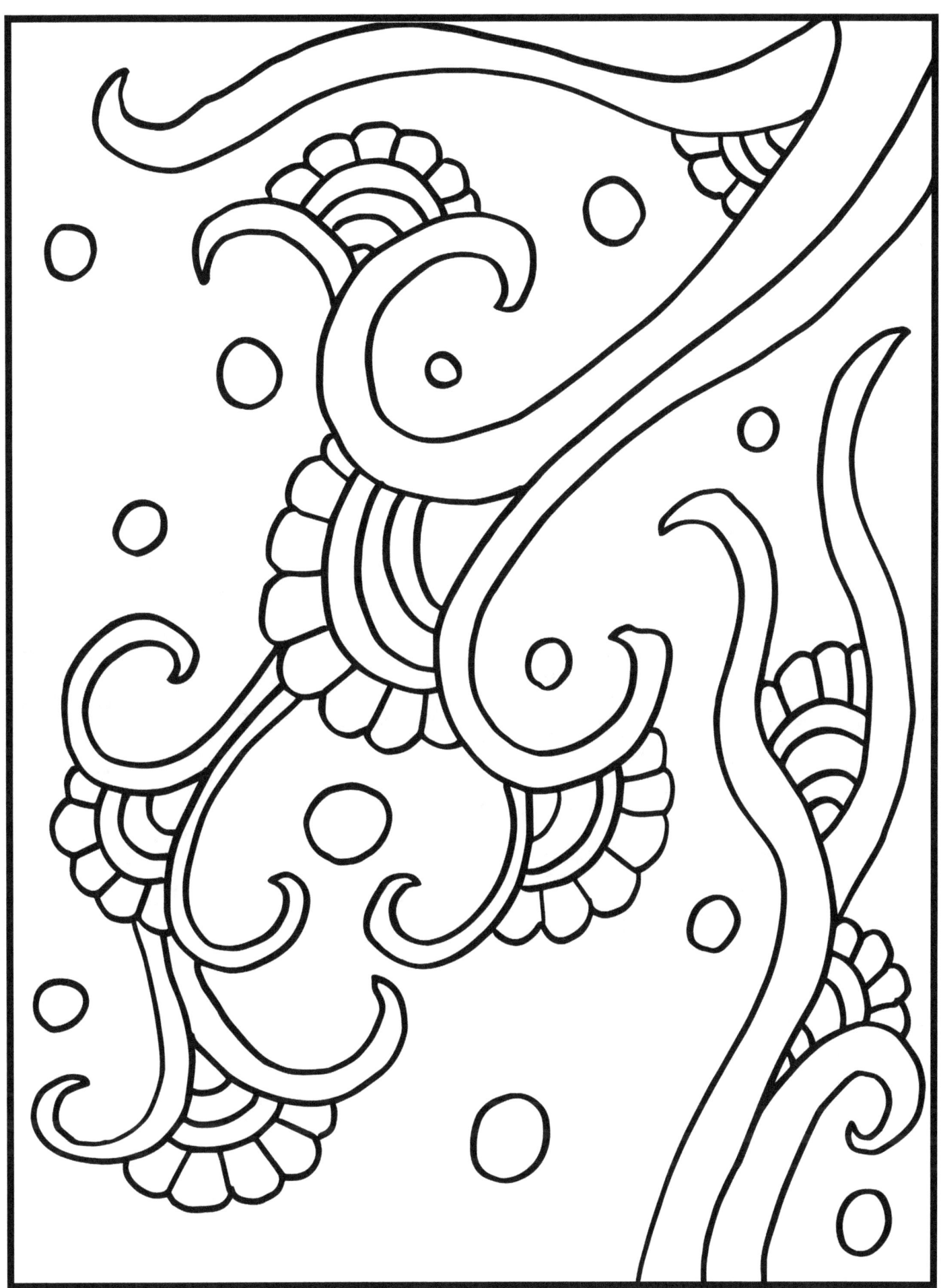

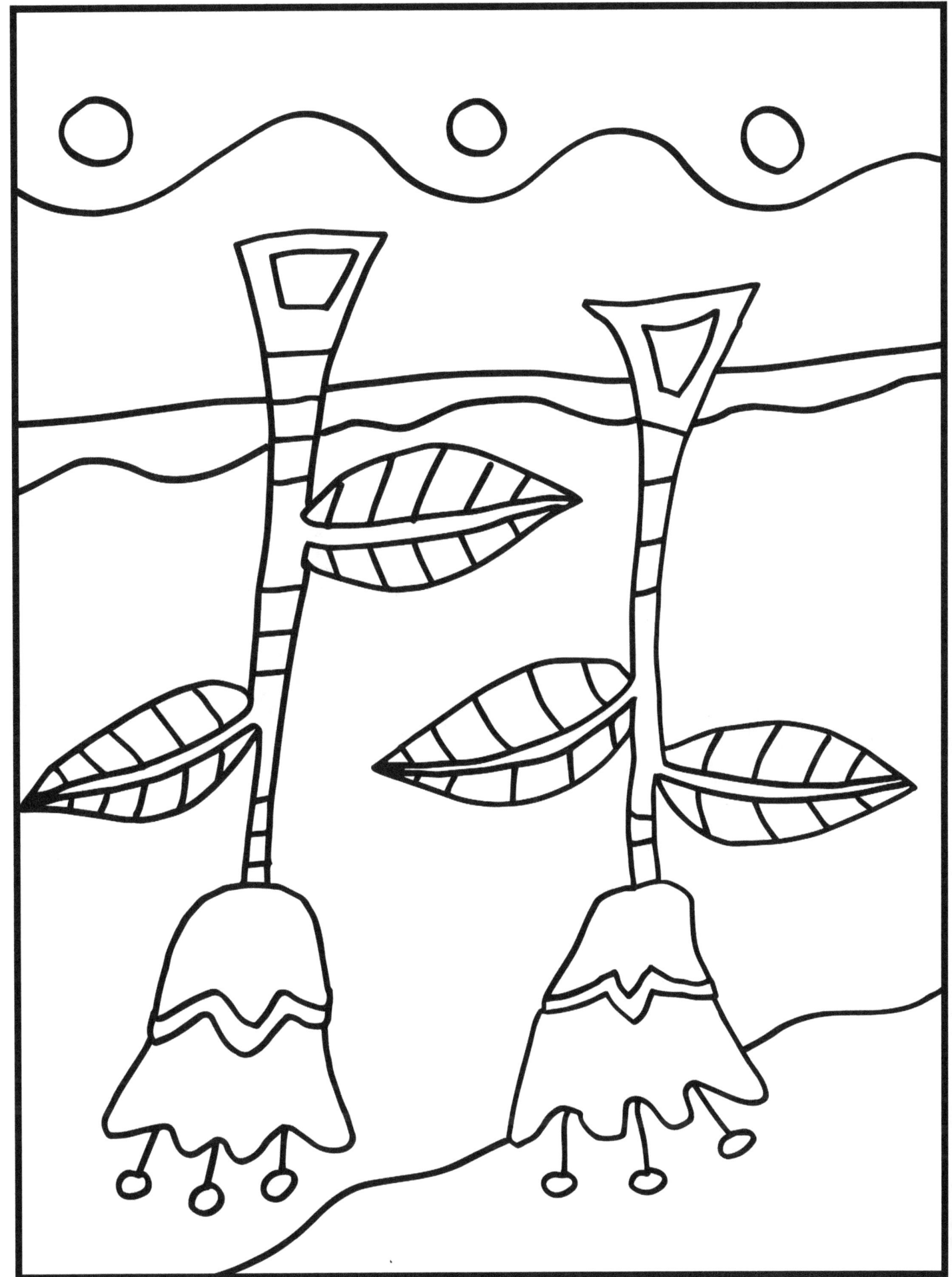

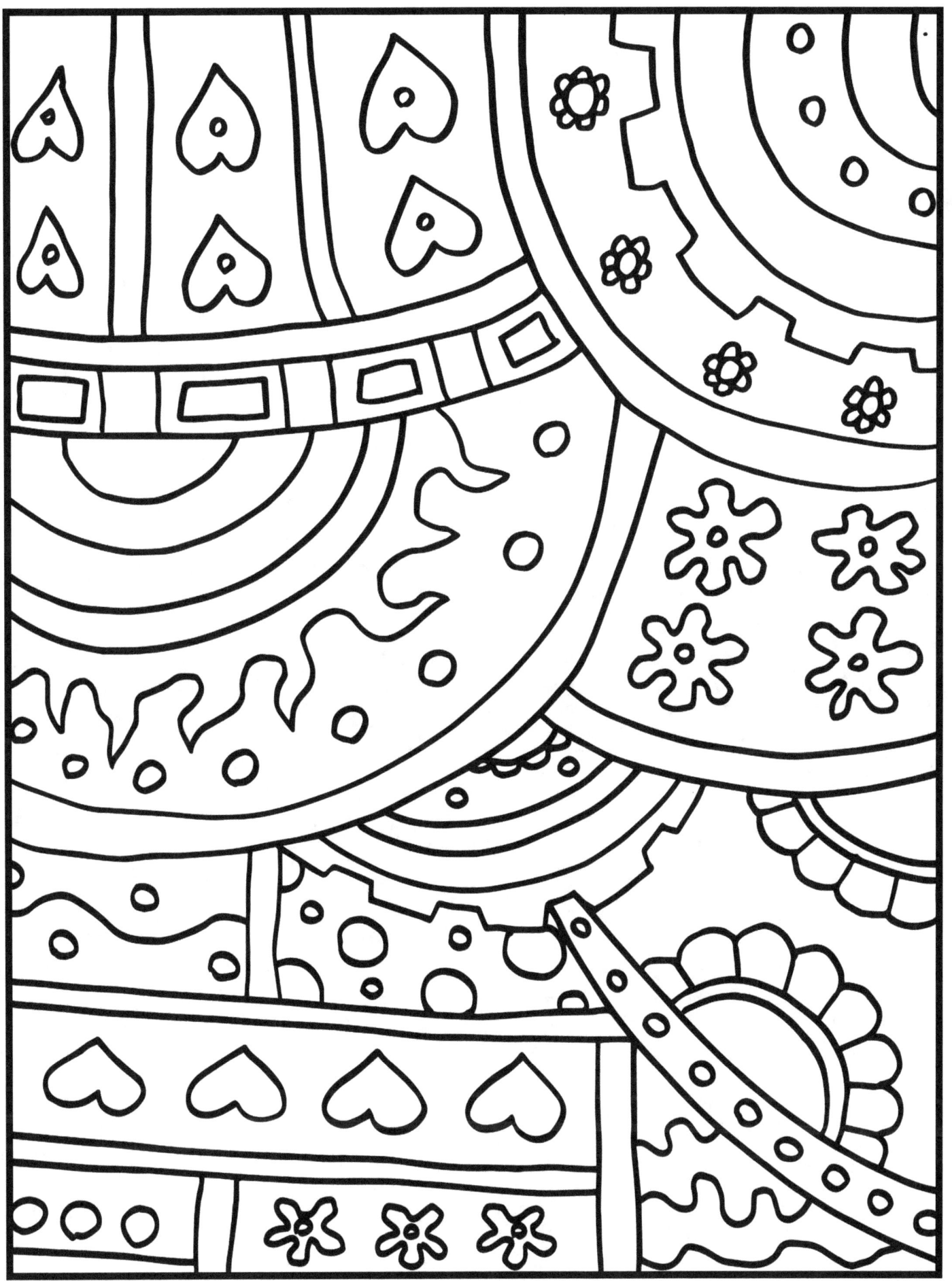

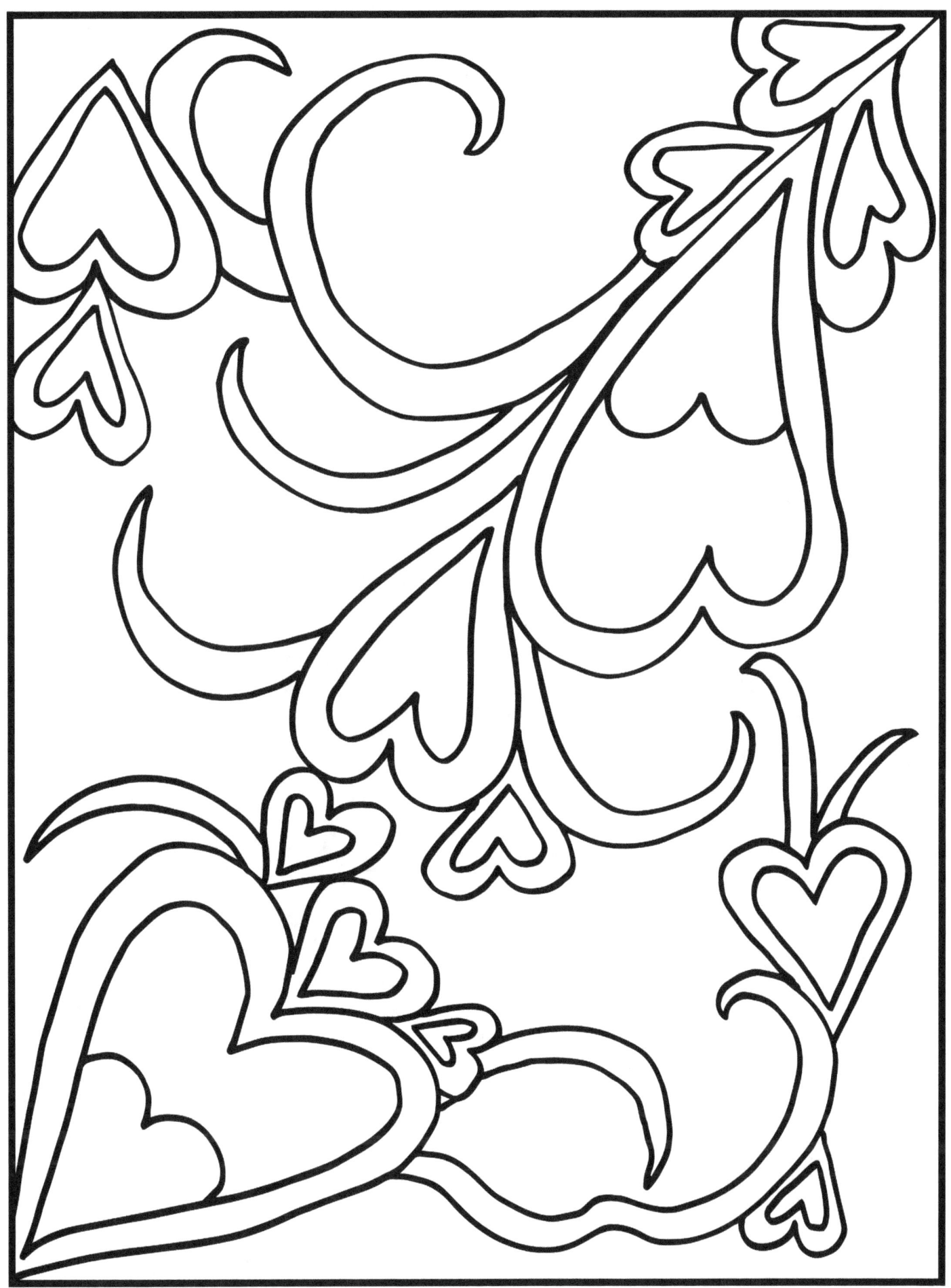

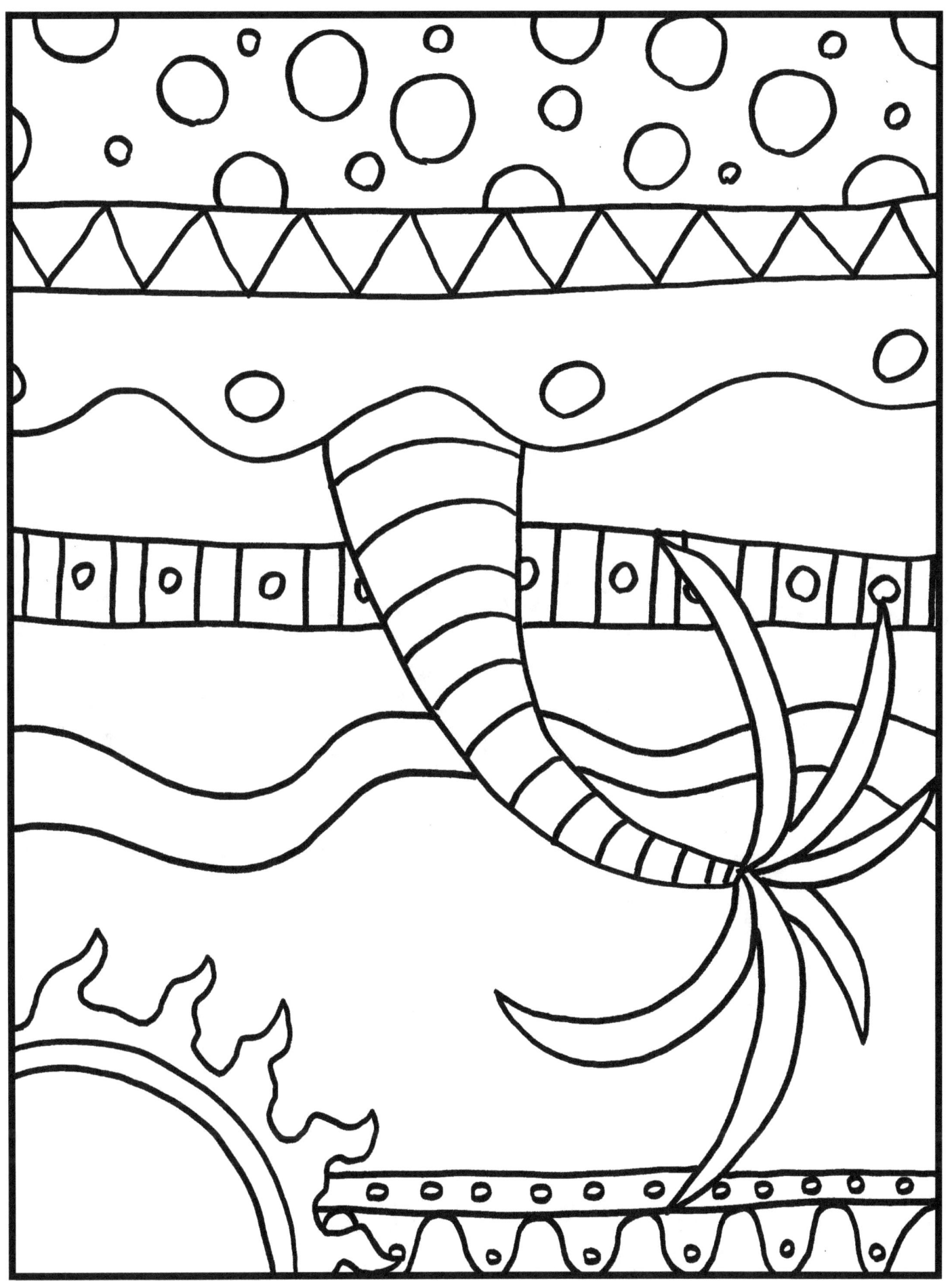

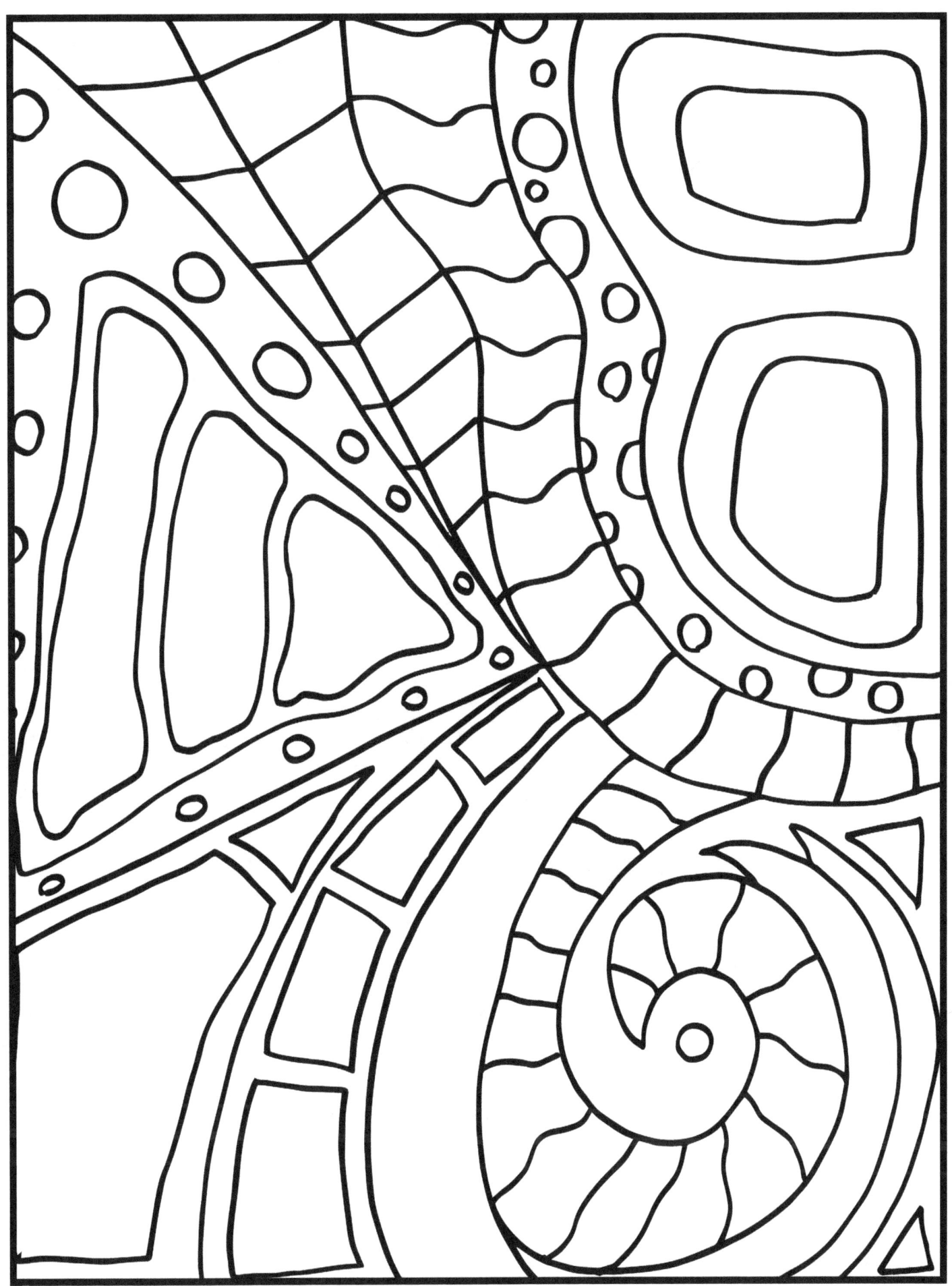

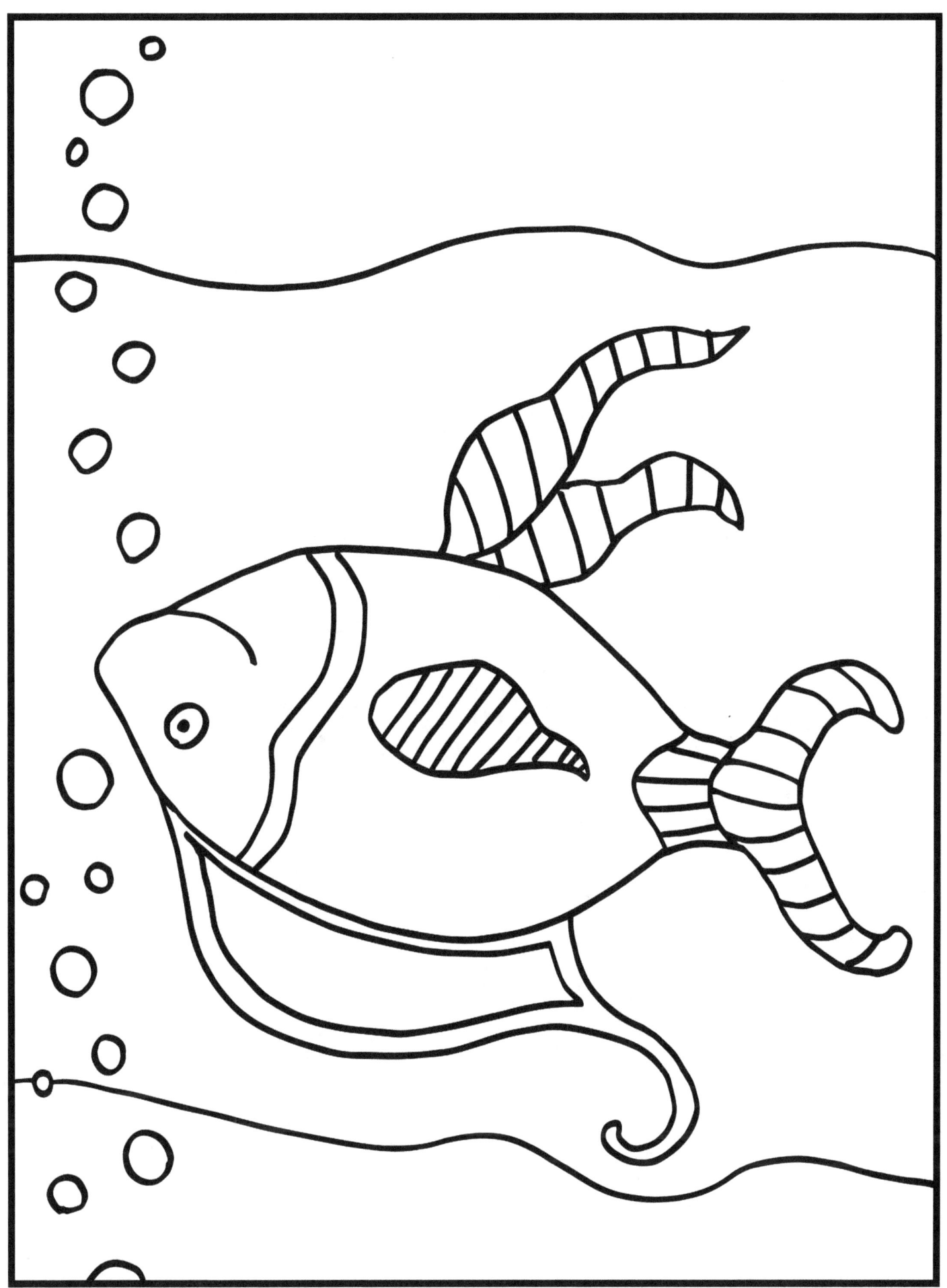

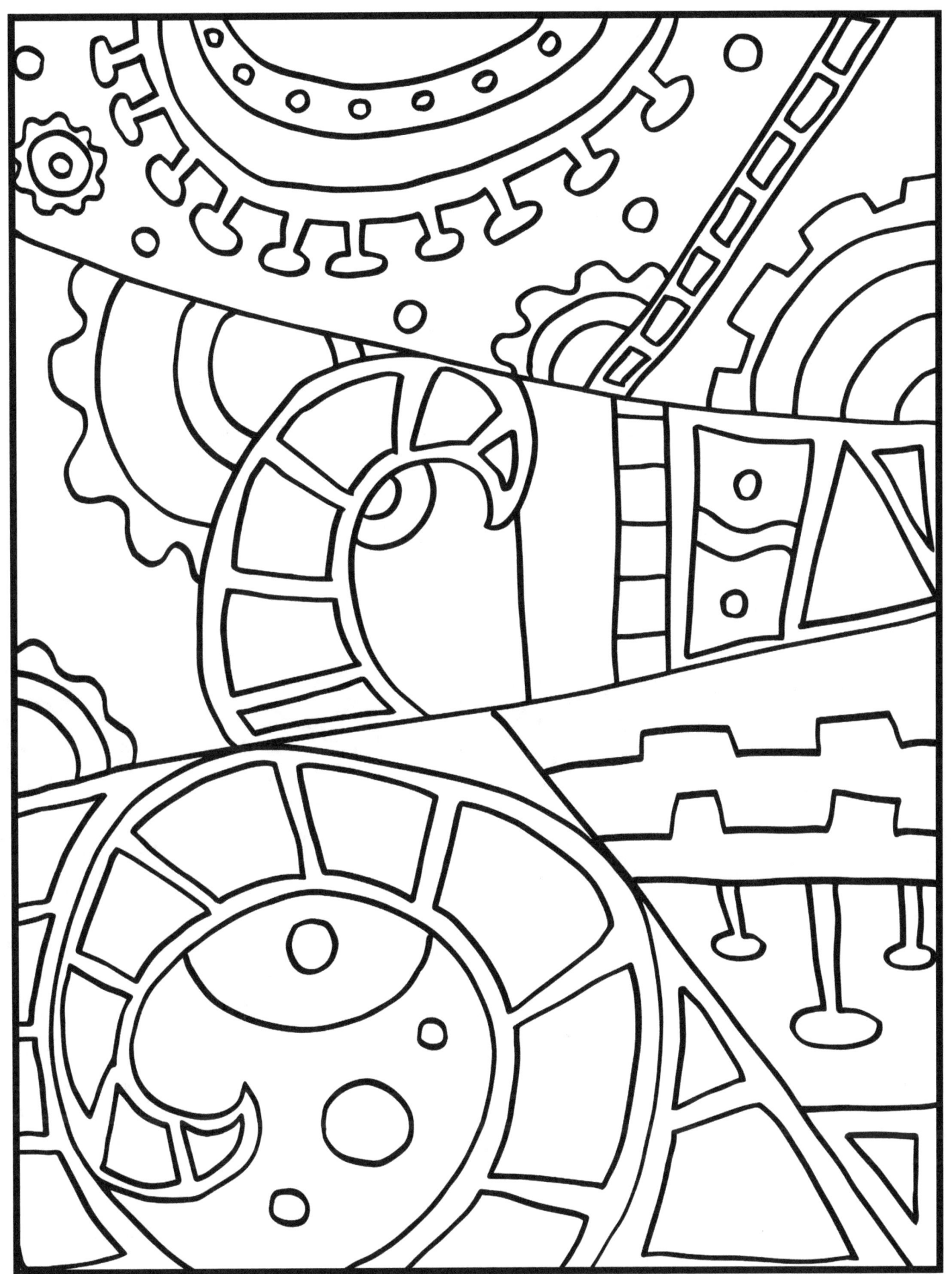

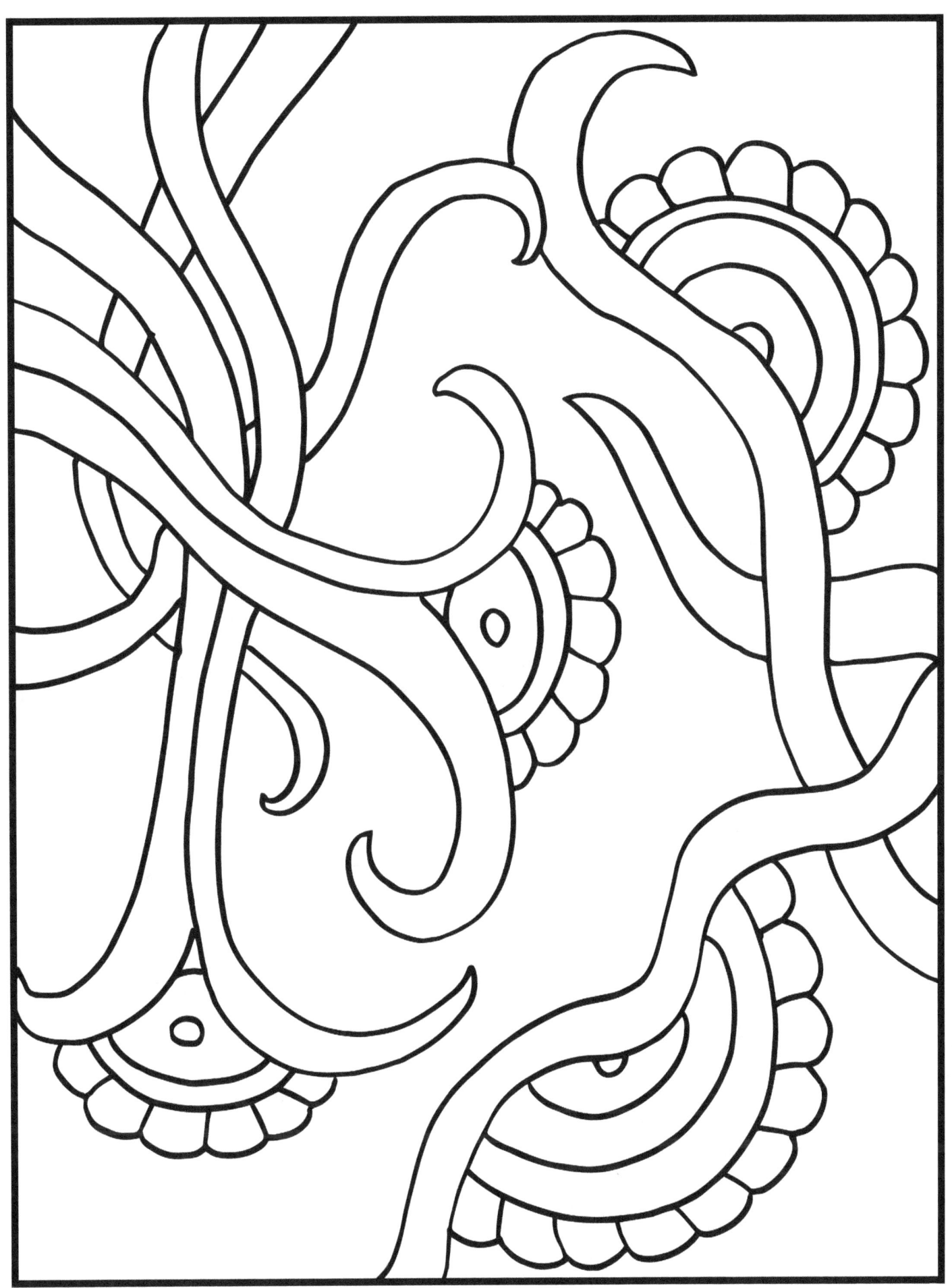

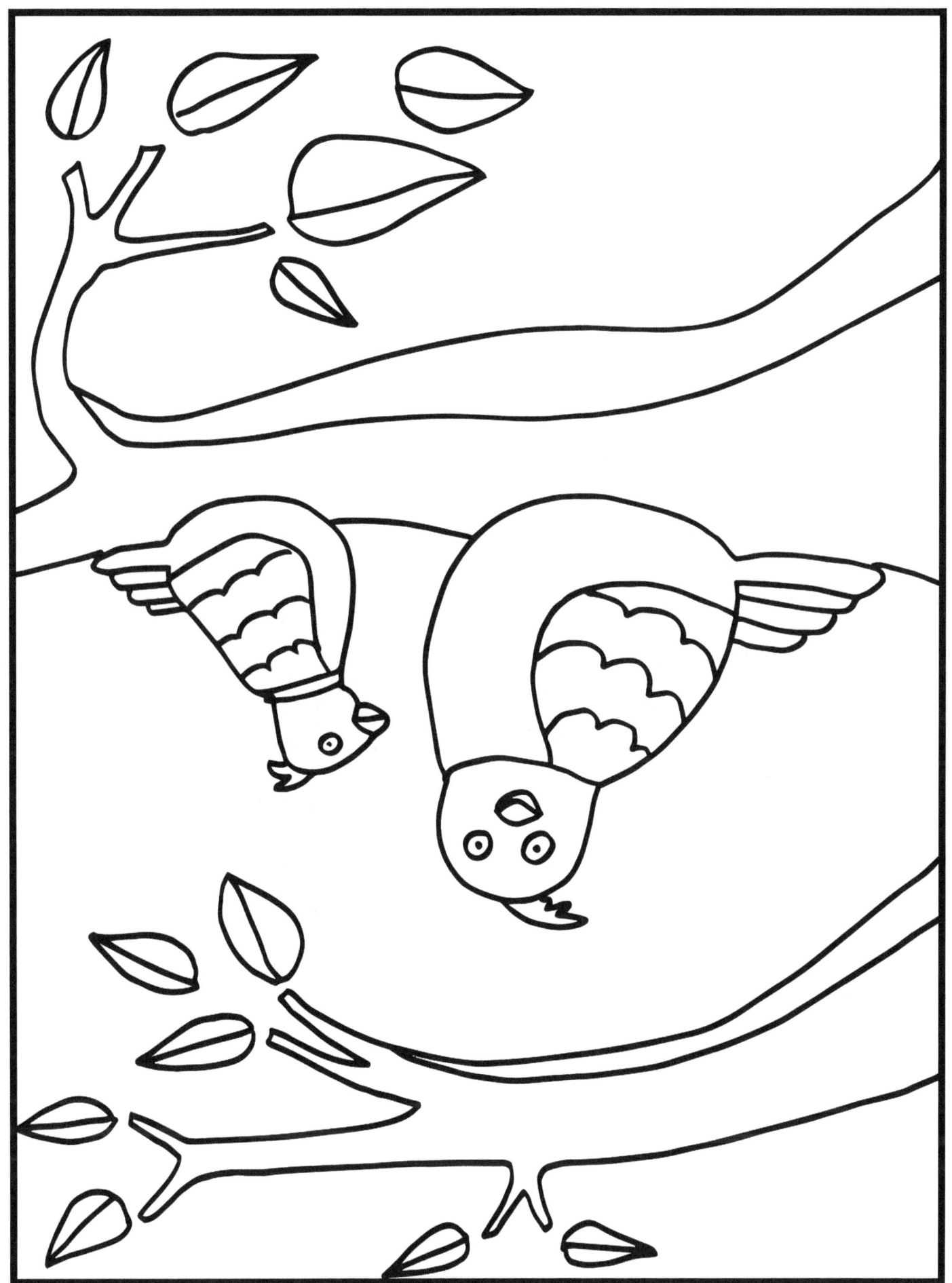

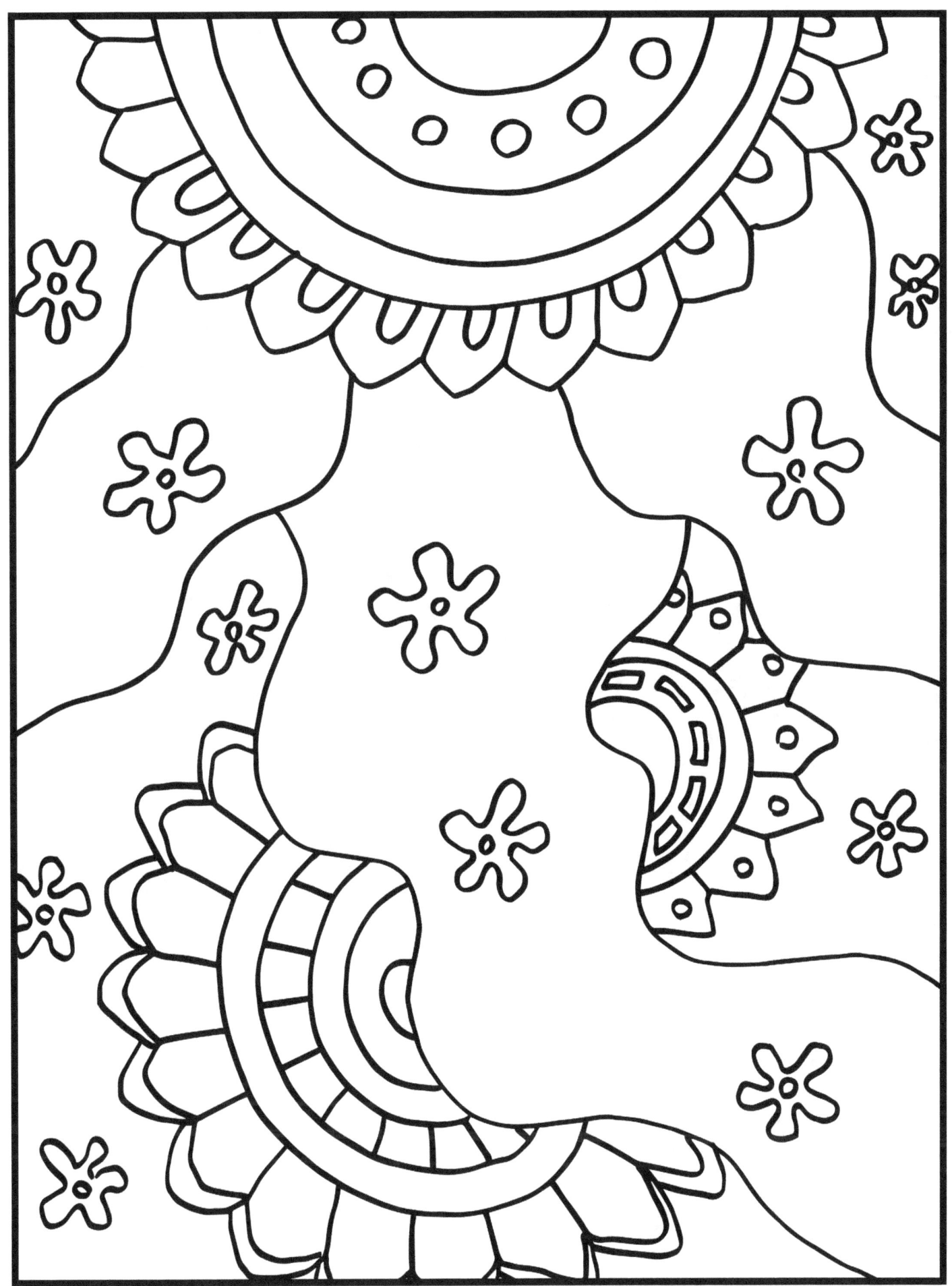

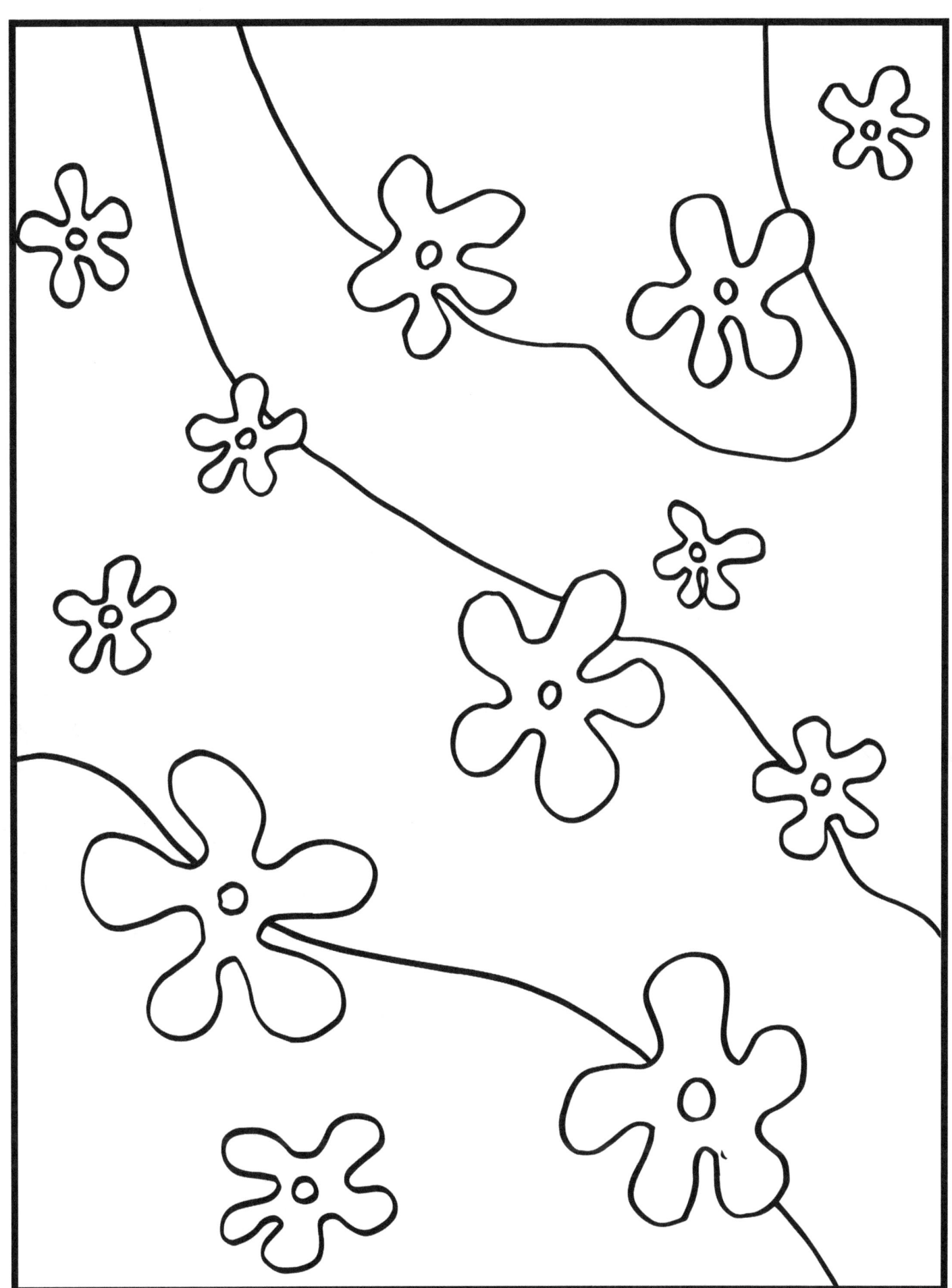

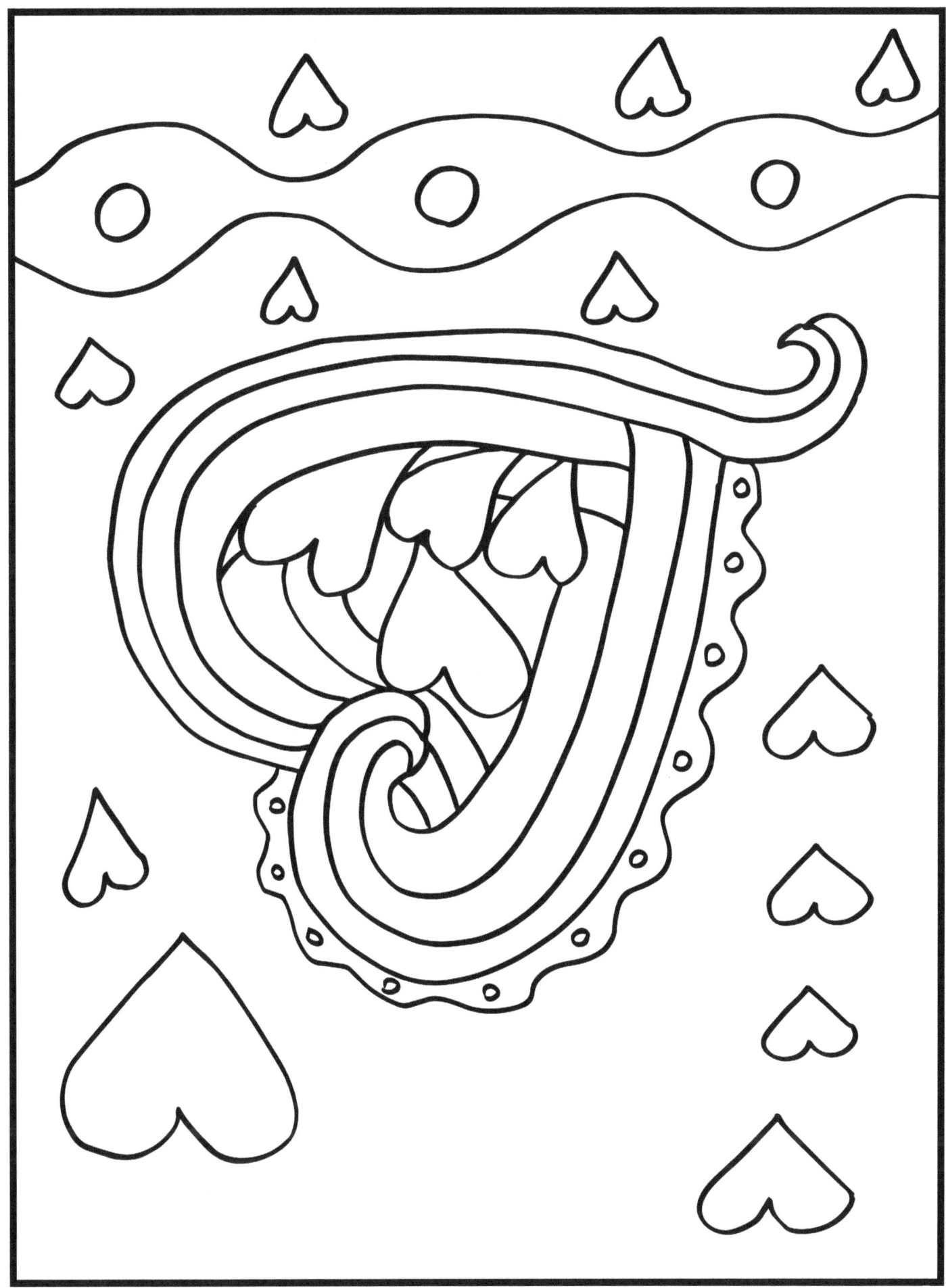

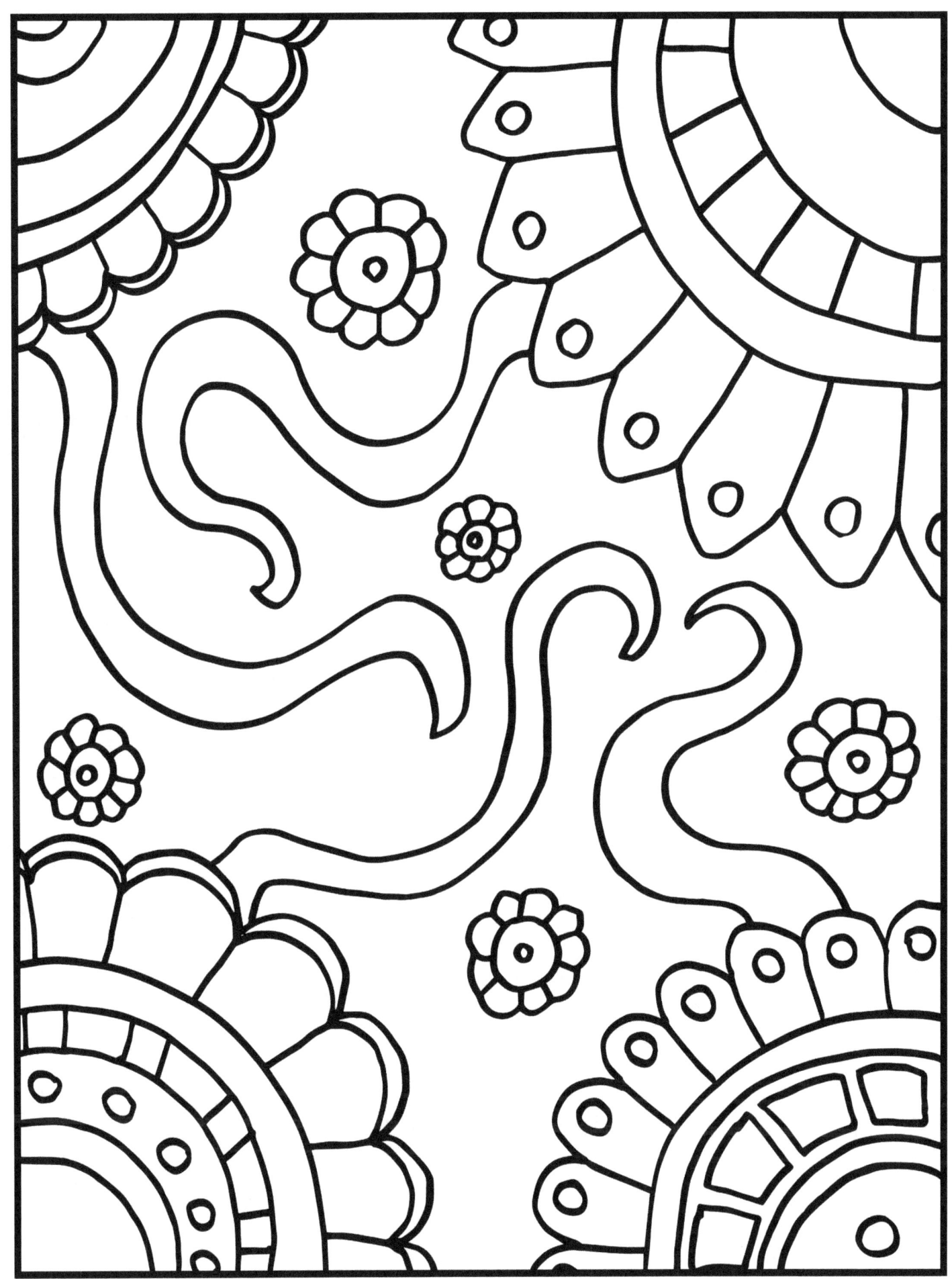

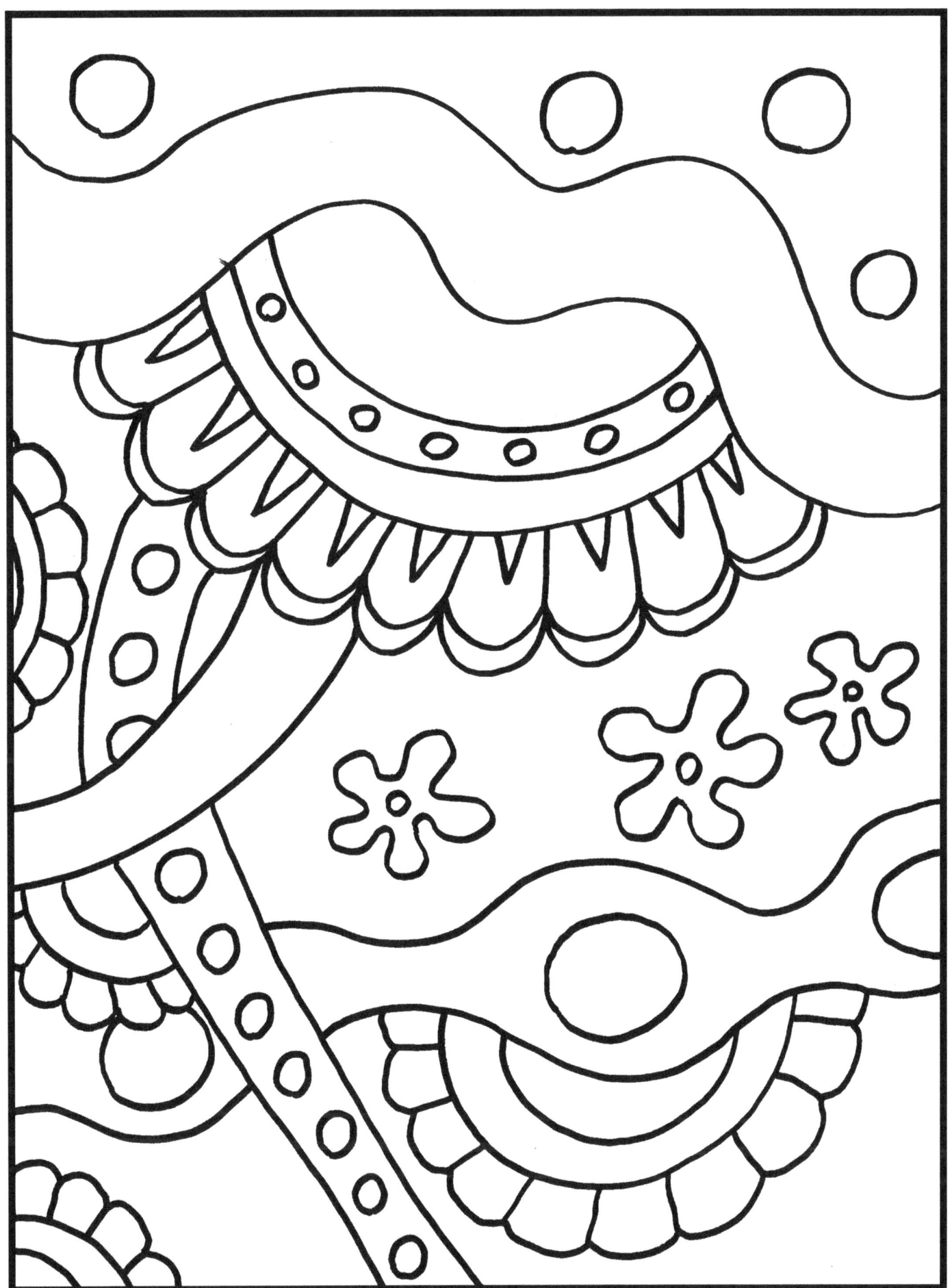

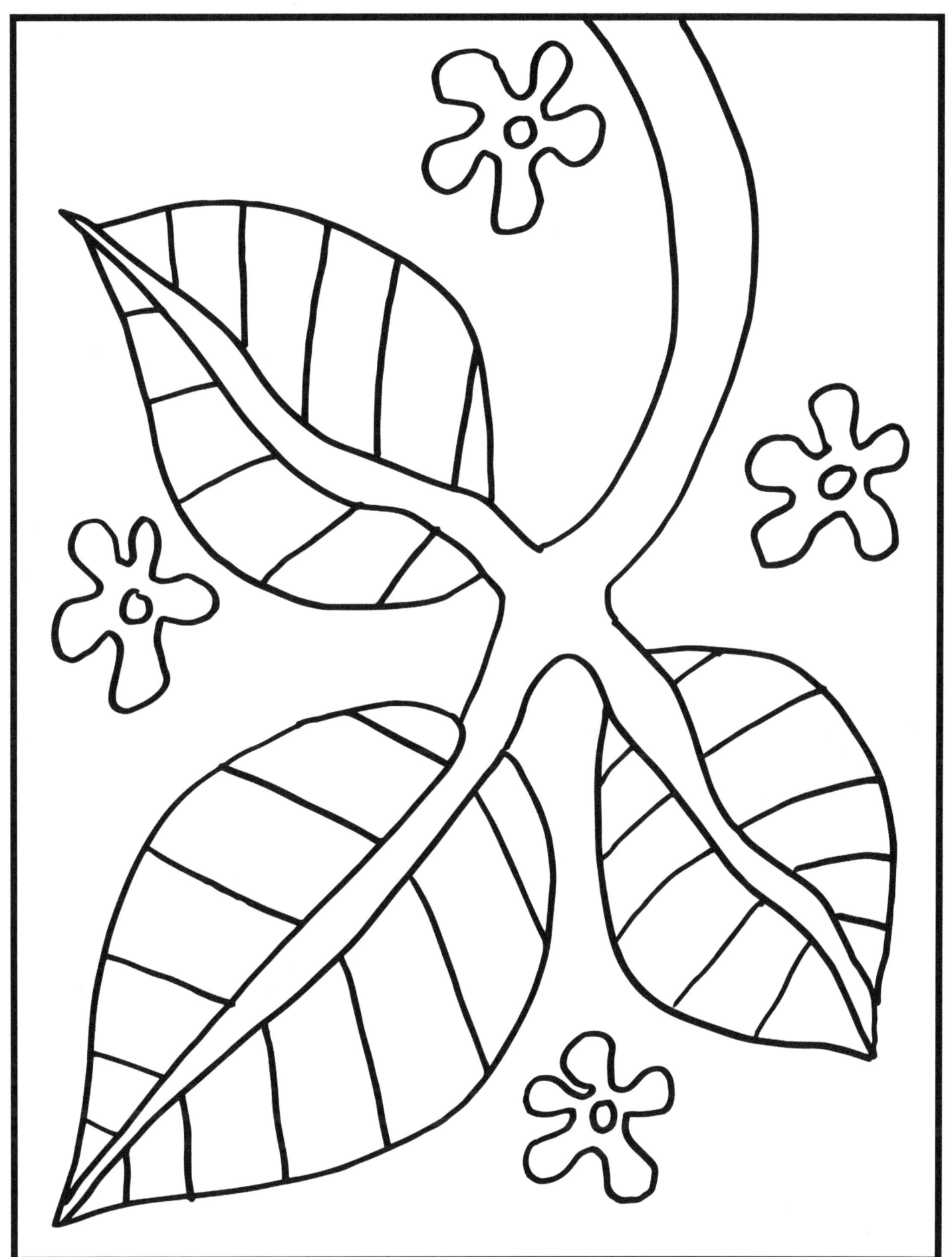

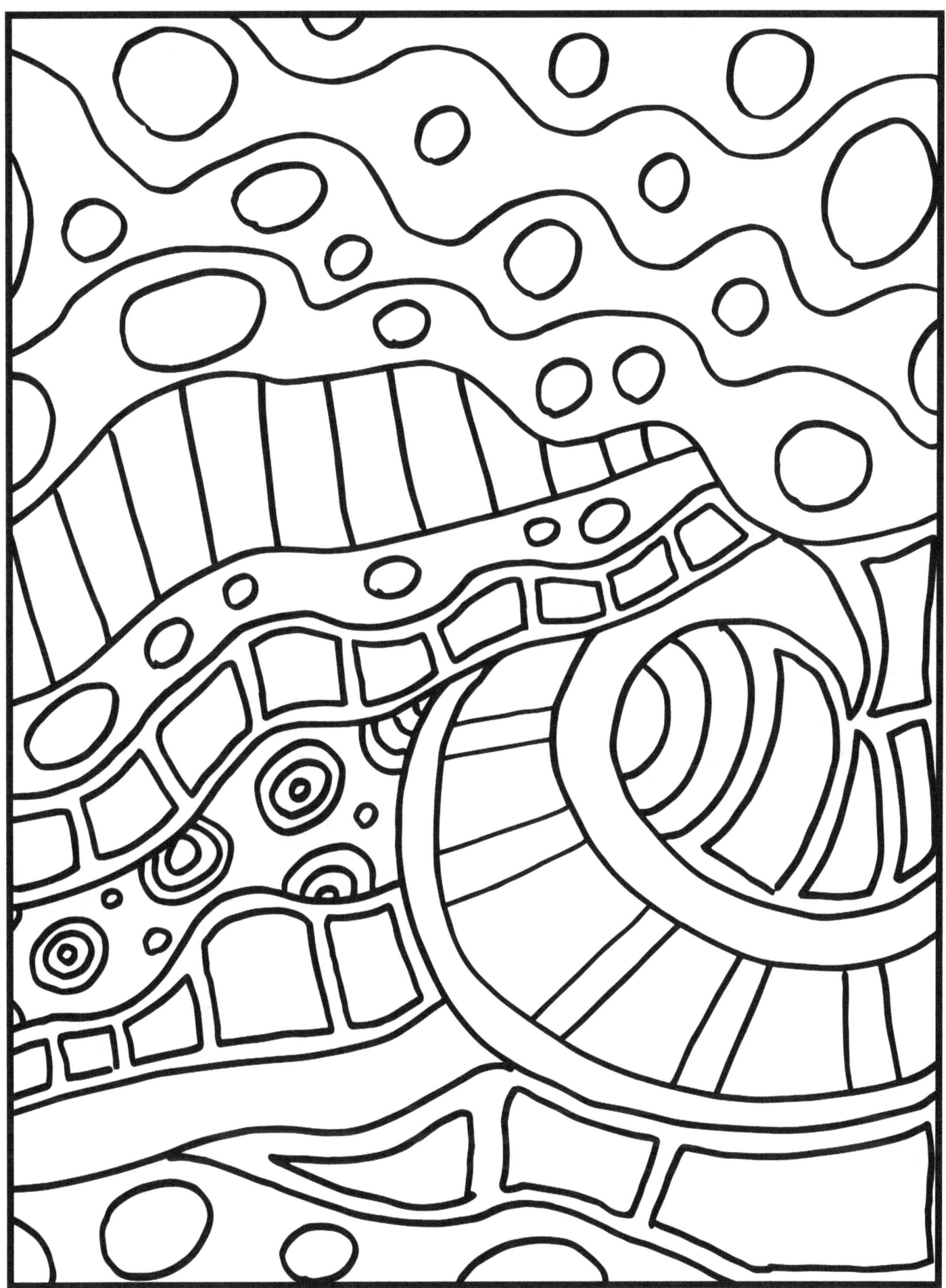

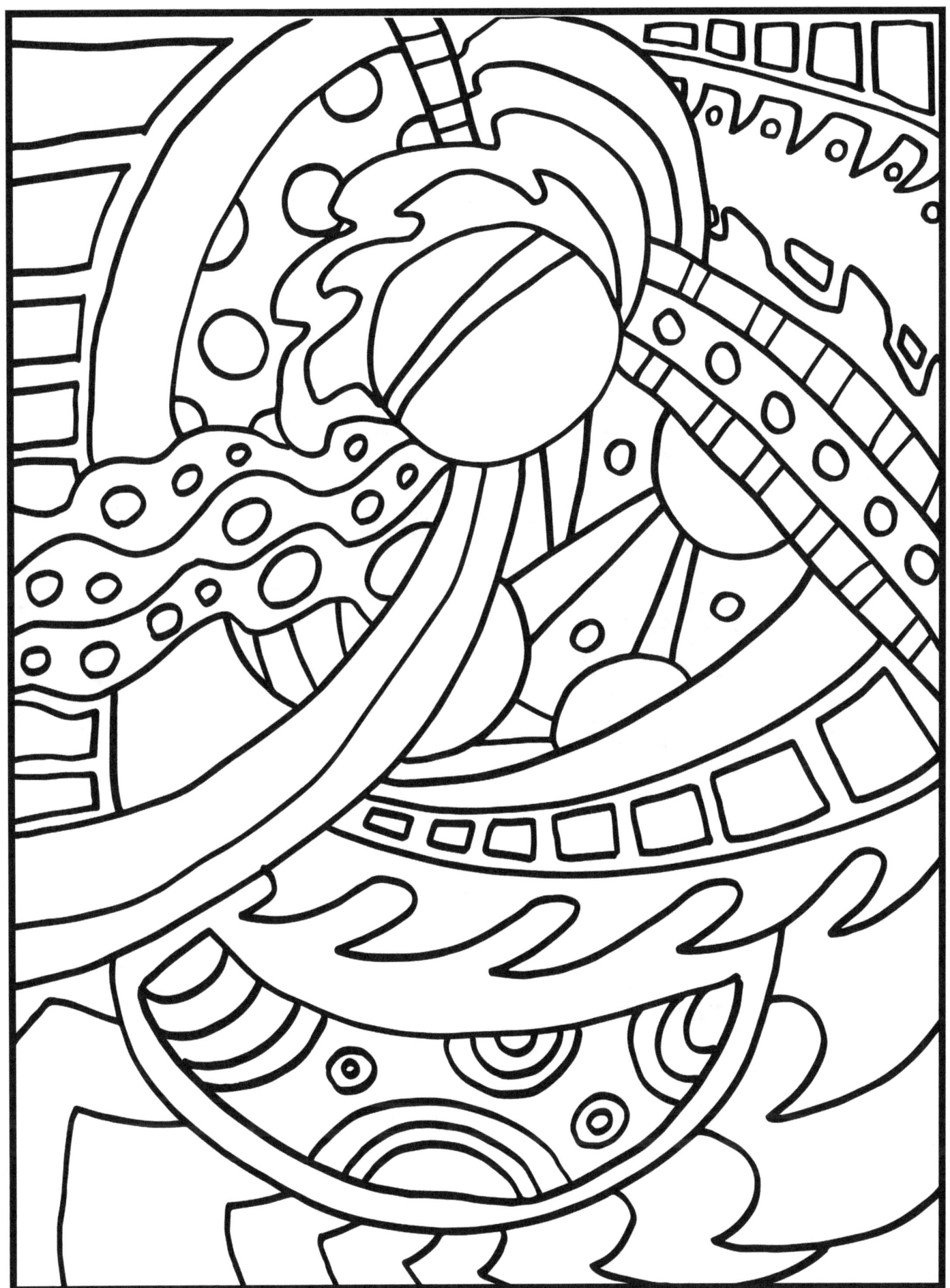

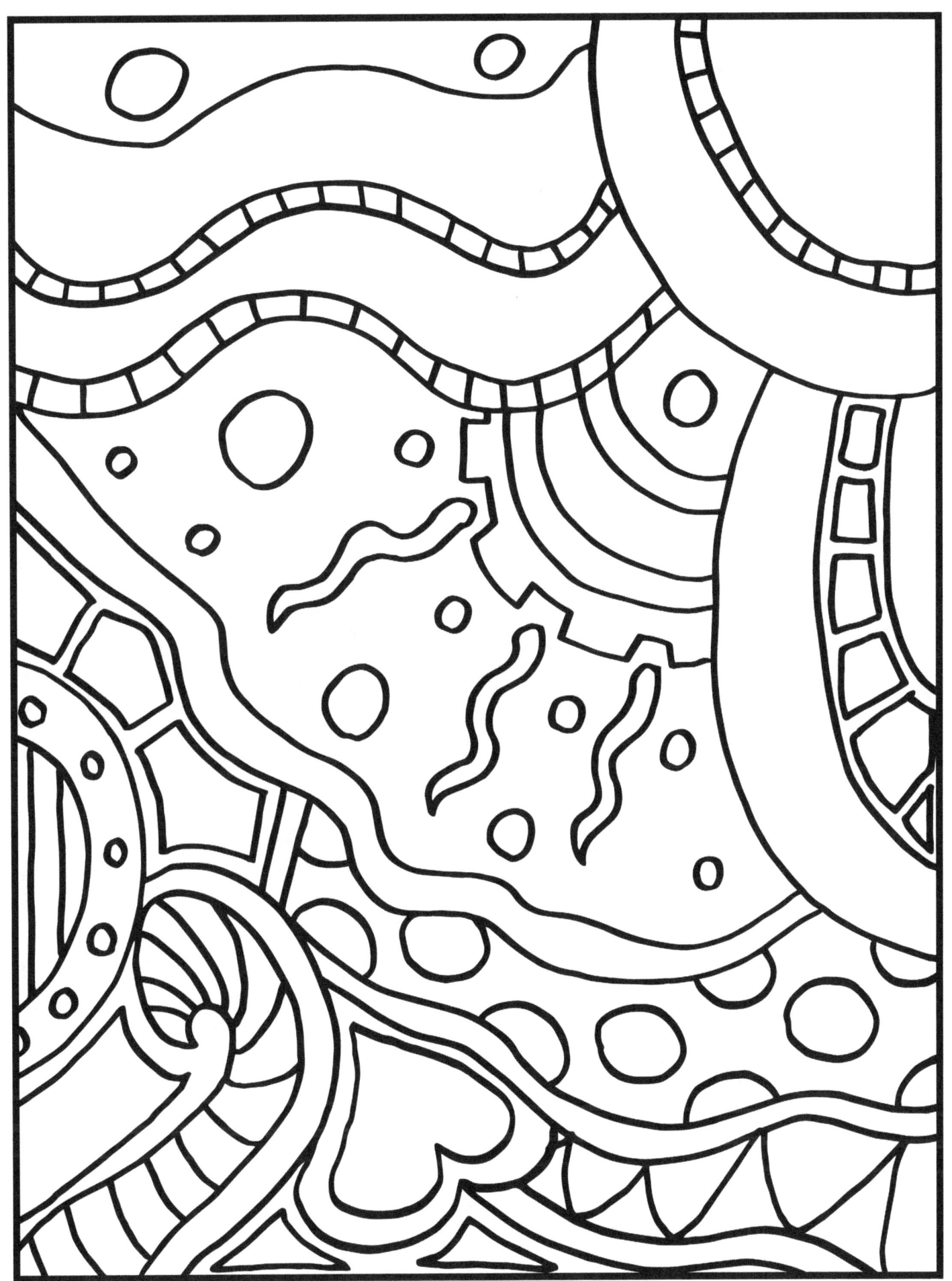

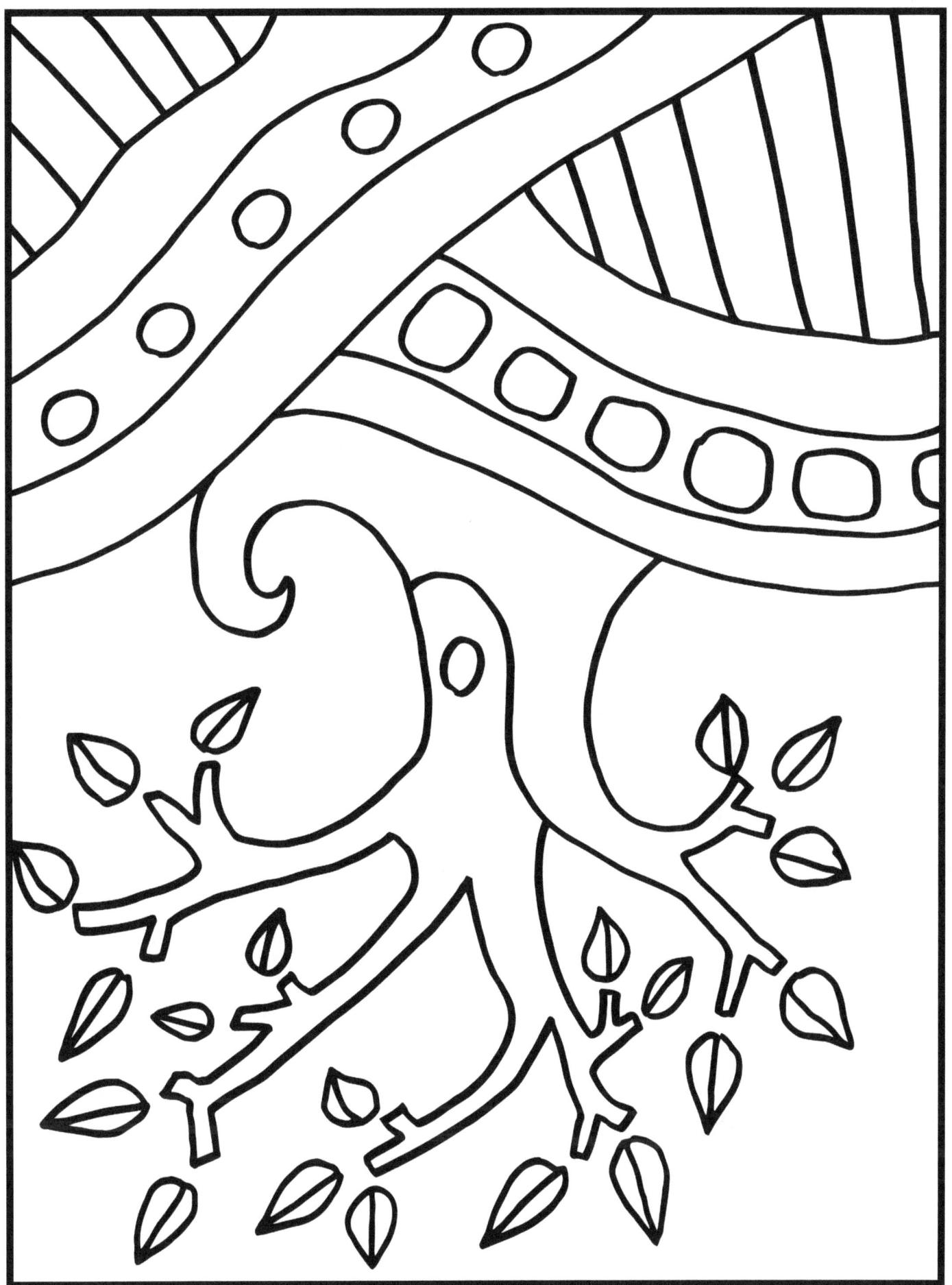

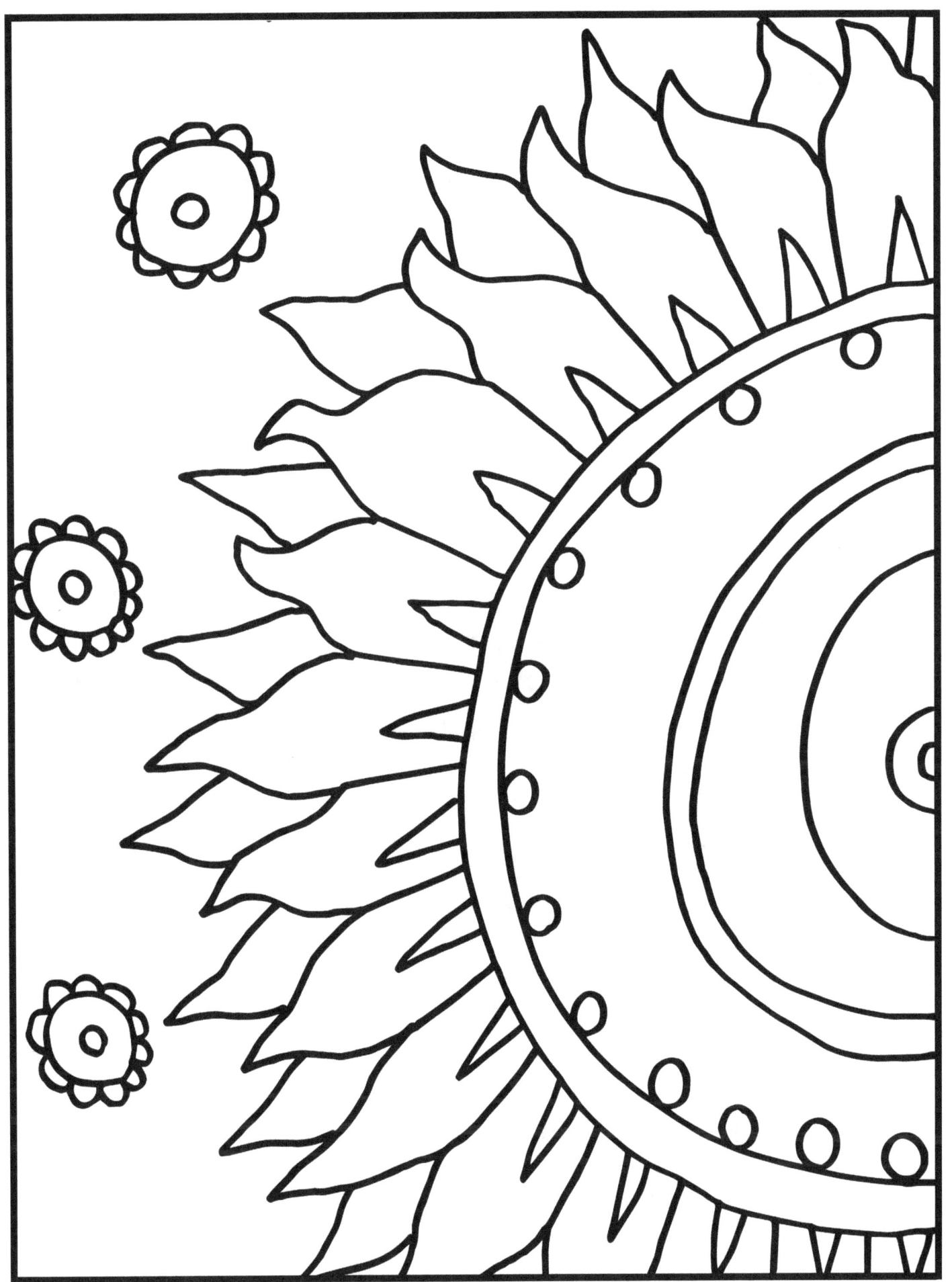

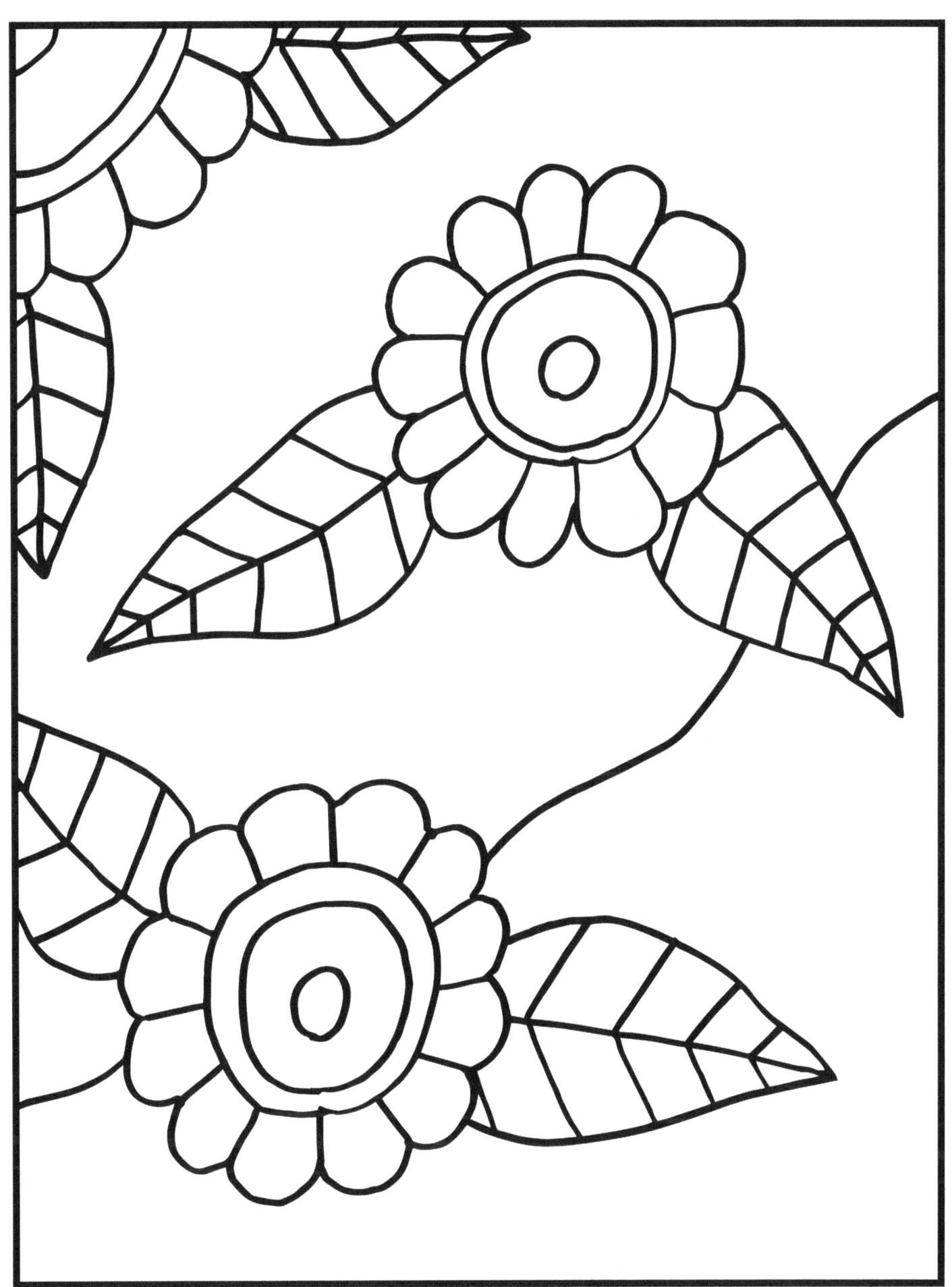

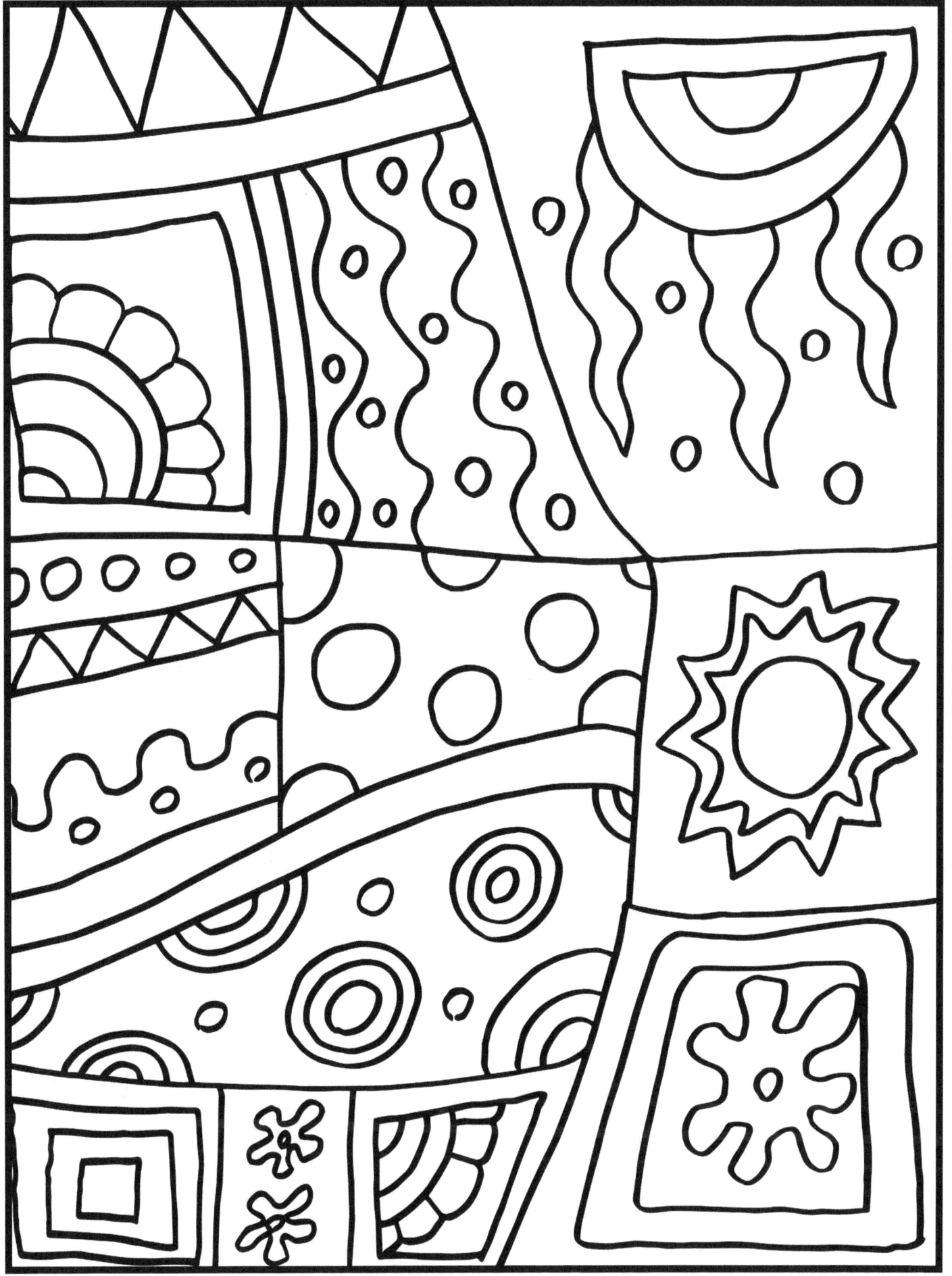

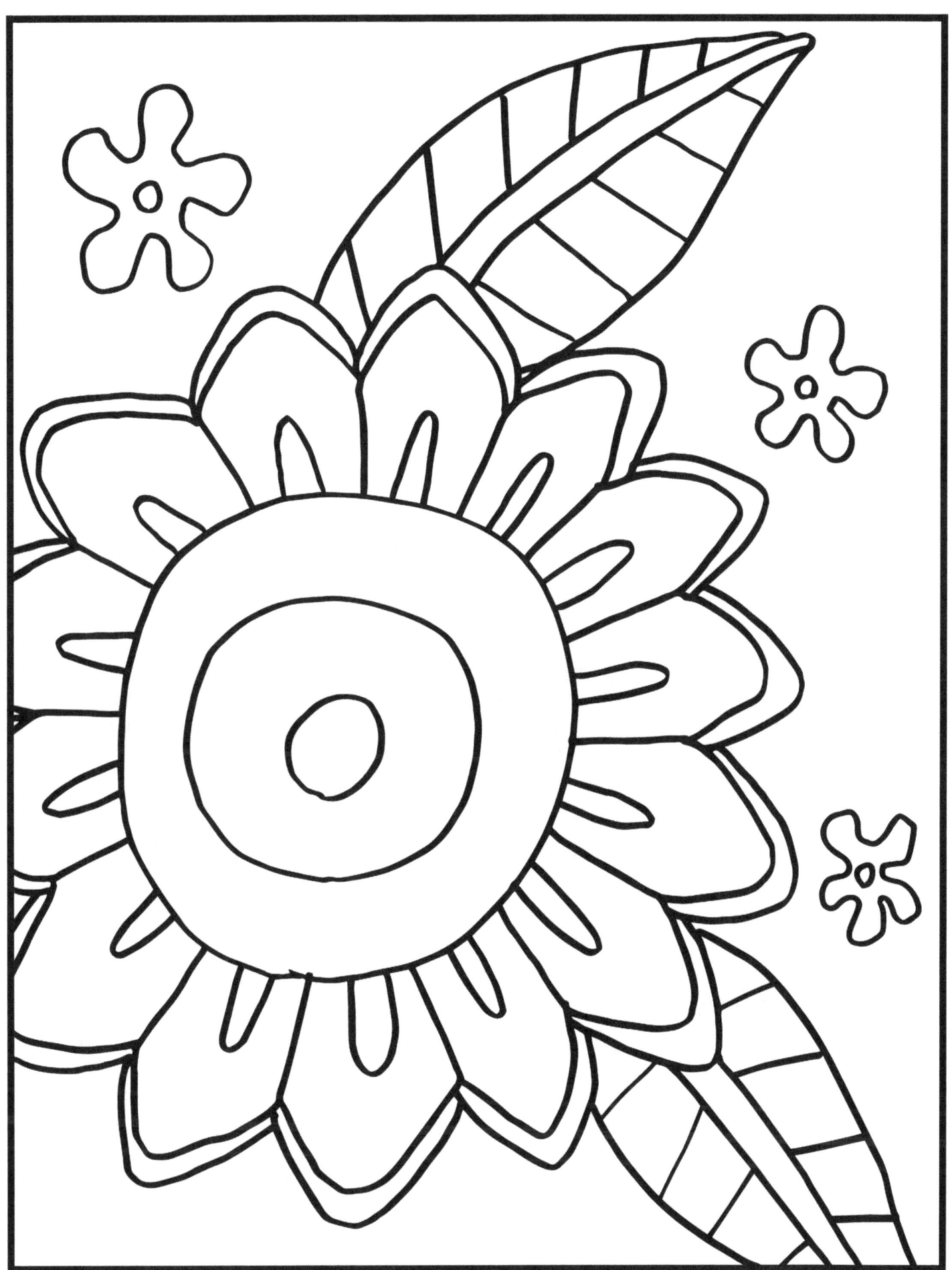

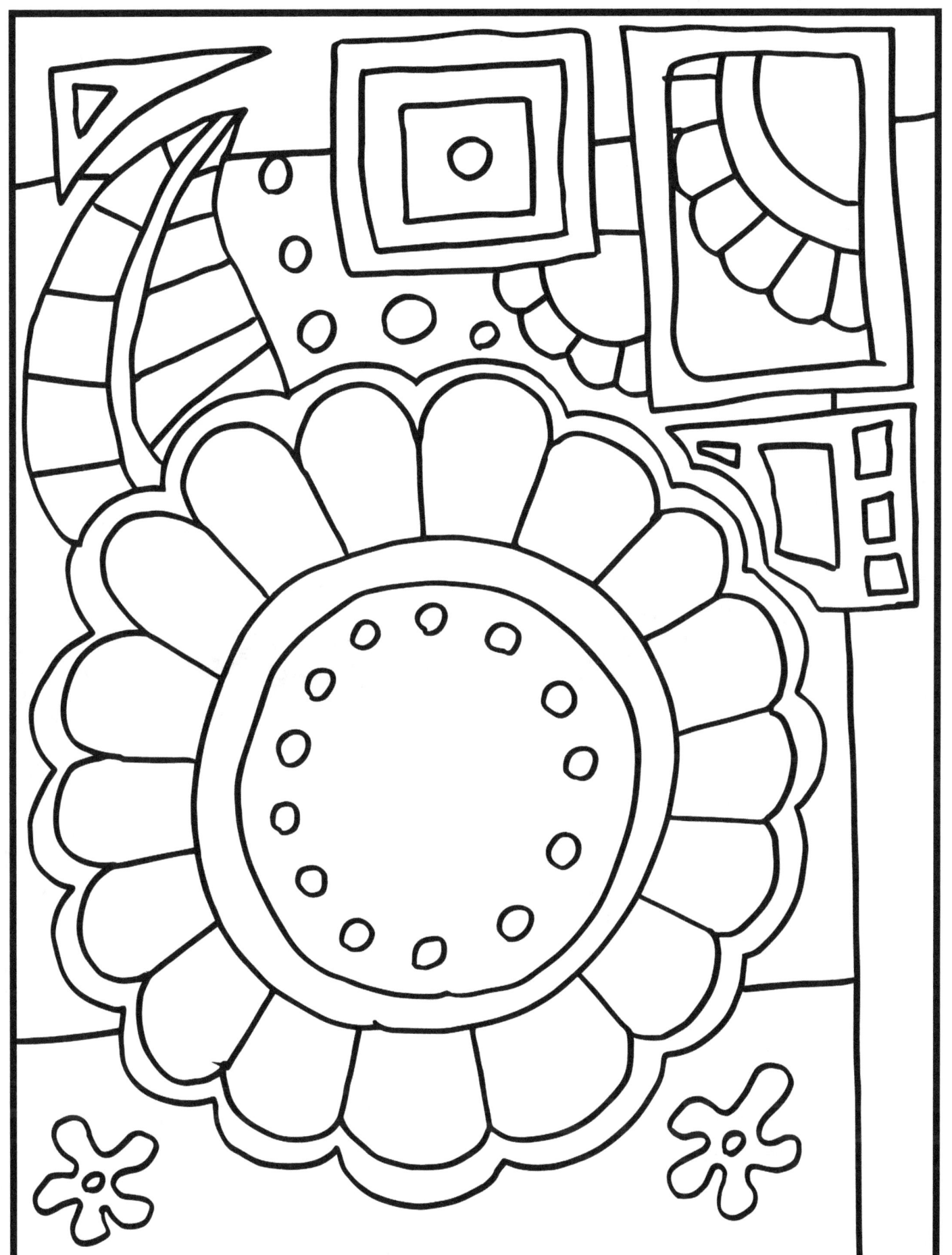

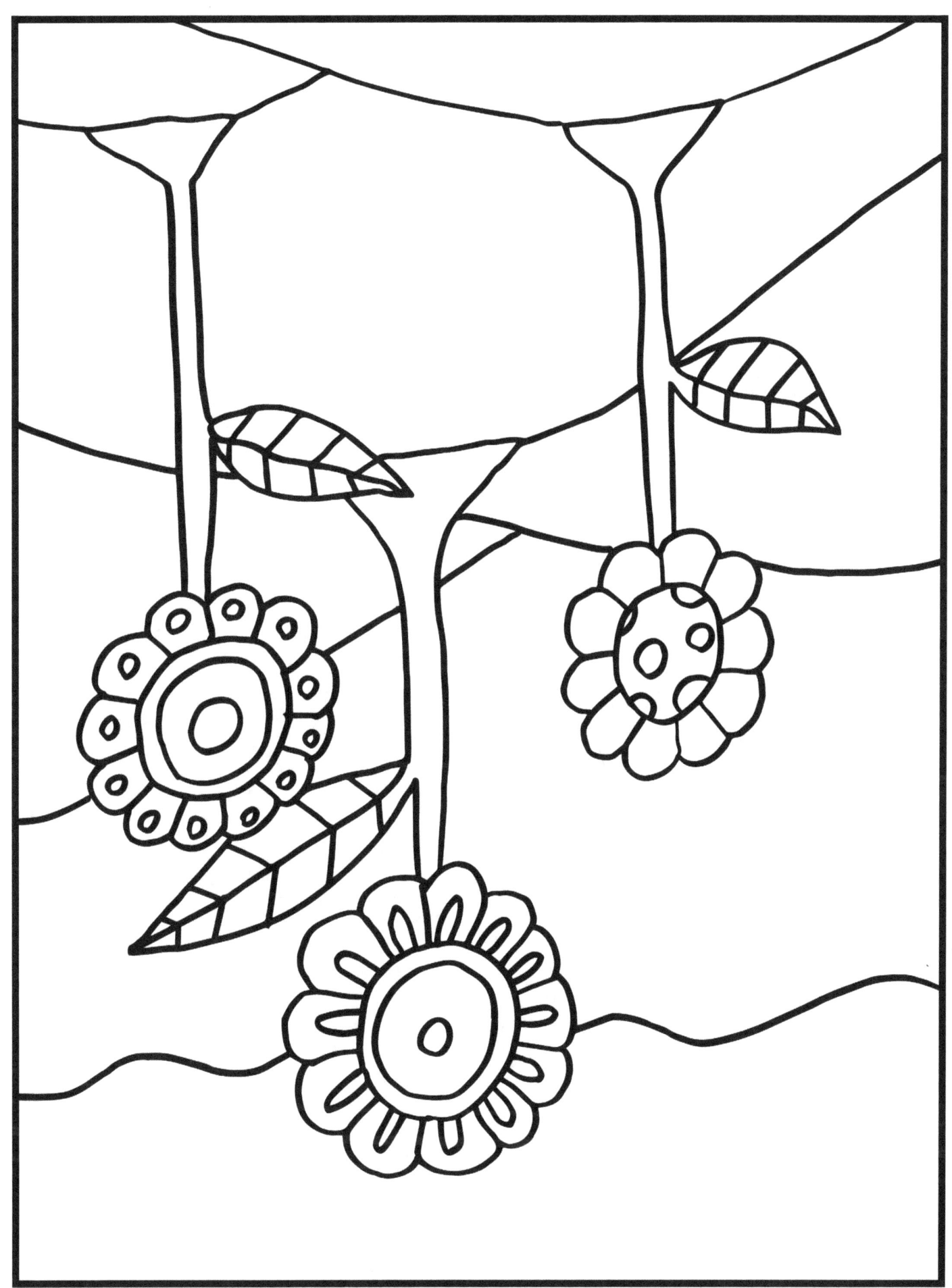

Also Available by Kimberly Garvey

- **Strange Designs** - An adult coloring book for everyone.

- **Strange Little Designs** - A mini/travel adult coloring book.

- **Simple Designs** - An adult coloring book with easier pages.

- **Simple Designs II** - An adult coloring book with easier pages.

- **Simple Little Designs** - A mini/travel sized book w/easier pages.

- **Magical Daydreams** - An adult coloring book for everyone.

- **It's Complicated** - A challenging book for the daring colorists.

- **The Fox Book** - A foxy coloring book for everyone.

- **SUPER Simple Designs -** SUPER easy adult coloring

- **SUPER Simple Designs II -** Another SUPER easy adult coloring

- **Playful Adventures** - An adult coloring book for everyone.

- **Random Designs** - Designs of various difficulty levels.

- **Alien Flowers From Another Dimension** - An adult coloring book for everyone.

- **I Love Hearts** - Heart themed coloring book for all.

- **Hours of Flowers** - An adult flowery coloring book.

- **Delightful Journeys**– Landscapes, places and animals.

KIMBERLYGARVEY.COM

PROTECTION SHEET

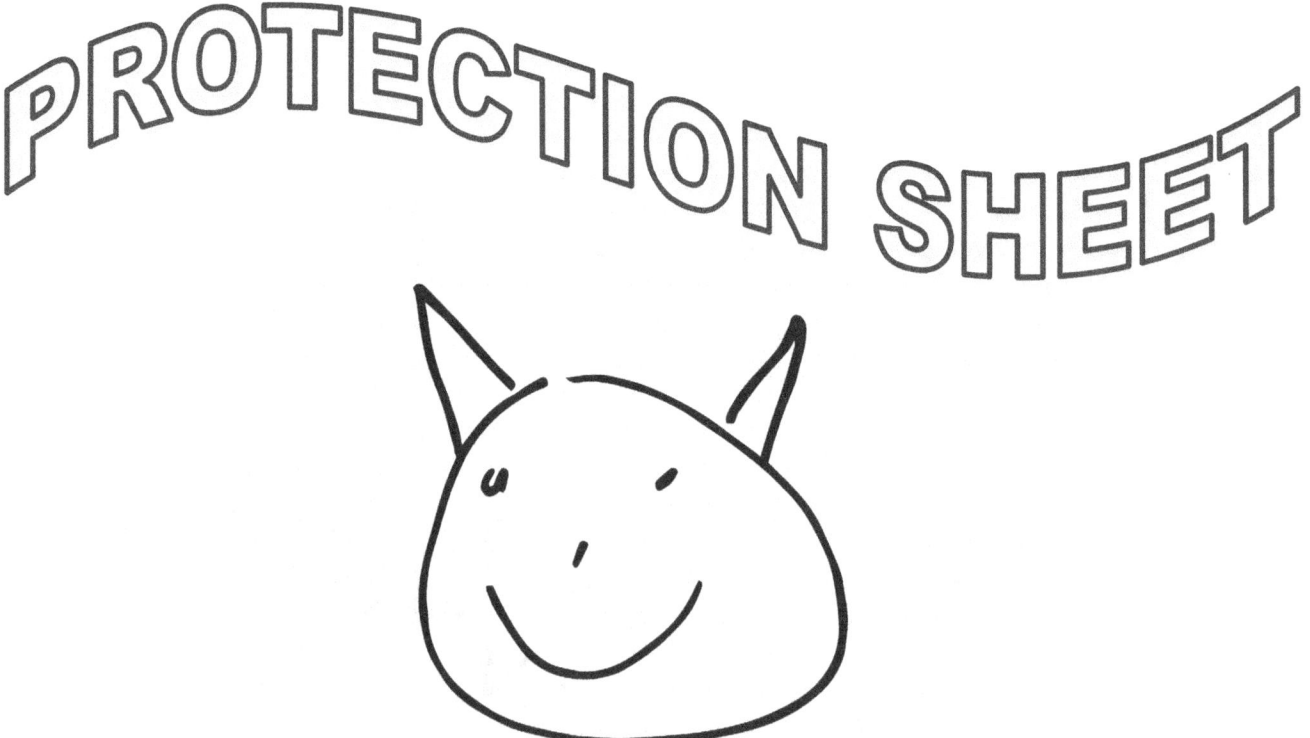

Place this page between coloring pages when using markers to prevent bleed-through.